Company Survival during Inflation

Company Survival during Inflation

A systematic approach to profit improvement

John Winkler

Gower Press

First published in Great Britain by Gower Press Limited,
Epping, Essex 1975

© John Winkler 1975

ISBN 0 7161 0309 5

Set in 10 on 12pt Press Roman by
PREFACE LIMITED
Salisbury, Wilts
and printed in England by
THE UNIVERSITY PRINTING HOUSE,
Cambridge

Contents

Illustrations   vii

Acknowledgements   ix

Introduction   xi

Part 1   Making a Profit During Inflation   1

1   How Inflation Distorts Business   3

2   The Systematic Approach to Profit Improvement   11

3   Methods of Creating Profit Improvement Ideas   19

4   Where to Look for Profit Improvements   29

Part 2   Inflation and Business Operations   41

5   Profit Improvement in General Management   43

6   Financial Accounting and Cash Management   55

7 Unfreezing the Cost Accounting Process   67

8 Improving the Purchasing Operation   77

9 Increasing the Value of the Output   87

10 Improving the Product Mix to Counter Inflation   97

11 Adapting Marketing Operations   111

12 Improving Productivity in Sales and Distribution   119

13 Pricing Strategy during Inflation   127

Part 3 Action Programmes for Profit Improvement   137

14 Action Steps to Implement the Systematic Approach to Profit
    Improvement   139

15 Check List for Profit Improvement Ideas   149

    Appendix: Pricing Restrictions   157

    Index   163

Illustrations

Figure

1.1 Inflation rates around the world   4
1.2 Inflation; industry costs and consumer prices   5
4.1 Example showing a substantial profit increase   30
4.2 The effect on profits of a small, combined improvement in sales,
     costs and prices   32
4.3 How one department's requirements may conflict with other
     department's   35
6.1 Adjusting profit before taxation from a historical to a current
     purchasing power basis   57
6.2 Summary of results and financial position adjusted for the effects of
     inflation   59
6.3 Forecasting cash flow   64
7.1 The danger of a high fixed cost business when the market turns down   72
7.2 How central cost allocations affect net profits   73
8.1 The effect of a 5% saving in materials costs   78
8.2 Supplier evaluation rating   82
9.1 A comparison of profitability between reducing labour costs or
     using spare capacity to increase output   92
10.1 Product elimination and profit improvement   102
10.2 Product elimination process   105
12.1 A comparison between cutting sales costs, and increasing sales with
     existing costs   123
13.1 How to make losses easily   128
13.2 A pricing strategy to cover inflation: a theoretical model   130
13.3 If the price is cut, how much more must be sold to break even?   134
14.1 Visual communication of data   145

To those few voices who cry, 'Stop this mad Western rush for material growth at all costs.'

Other books by John Winkler:

Marketing for the Developing Company
Winkler on Marketing Planning

Acknowledgements

To Miss Dare, the chief librarian at the British Institute of Management, for her help in scouring the lesser documented areas of the subject; to Mr Robert Smith of Gower Press for his help in getting the strategy and structure right; to four ladies around the offices of the Winkler Marketing Group who either handled the research or typed the manuscript, Mrs Reifet, Mrs Murray, Mrs Steed and Miss Mitchell; and to my family for walking about on tiptoe while the writing was on — my grateful thanks.

Introduction

Introduction

Very slowly, but very surely, the world's consumption of certain materials upon which Western societies have come to depend is outstripping their supply. Some resources cannot be replaced fast enough; others cannot be replaced at all.

This is a relatively new situation for the world to cope with and observers have noted its awesome implications for the future of mankind. This book covers a somewhat smaller canvas. Firstly, it attempts to show that the link between materials shortage and rising inflation has an impact upon the effective running of a manufacturing business. Secondly it surveys the stresses caused by rising inflation upon the various business functions. Finally it makes tentative suggestions as to avoiding action which a business manager could take.

Inflation, with rates running at levels of 10% or 20% is thoroughly disruptive. Its impact upon costs is uneven in timing and in strength and consequently can lead to a cash shortage crisis even in a well-run and profitable company. The impact of inflation on markets is uneven. Some customers will seek new cheaper sources of supply, the level of total demand in other markets will be reduced as buying power erodes. Other firms will find new growth opportunities as a result of inflation.

The impact of inflation production can be very ugly. As the buying power of salaries and wages drops, so staff for low-paid jobs will be hard to recruit, wage negotiations will become more intractable; industrial relations will deteriorate, production will stop and products on the market will be short. In the hardest hit industries the result could be rising unemployment and social unrest.

This is not a book about theoretical business economics. It attempts to trace the way in which decisions are made and money is spent and to show in a practical manner how this might be improved. It is more concerned with the way people are managed and the way they think than with analytical techniques or measurement systems. A method for starting a Profit Improvement Programme is proposed which has been proved successful in many companies in different countries; rising inflation is a world wide problem after all. Although the background to the book is the country which should know more about dealing with inflation than most, the United Kingdom, it is also appropriate for an audience stretching across the world, from the Americas to the Far East.

In particular, the book is intended for senior and middle managers in manufacturing enterprises with the purpose of indicating where they could probe for weaknesses in their various business operations. Some relatively novel ideas are explored, for example, purchasing techniques when sellers are reluctant to supply in conditions of shortage, an indexed pricing plan to cover inflation, a method of tight budgeting, and product rationing strategies during shortages. The most important aim is to persuade management to take considered and planned action to improve profit performance. Most managers know where extra savings are to be made in a crisis but, either there is difficulty in passing them through the various organisational levels, or the saving is a one-shot surgical operation.

It must be realised however, that inflation is here for a long time to come, bringing continuous disturbance in its wake. What is needed is a continuous plan for operating an entire business more tightly, allowing for perhaps an overall zero growth rate in the short term, meanwhile developing new business in profitable areas and cutting back less profitable operations. The book concerns exactly this type of 'push and pull.'

Profit improvement programmes are good, cost reduction programmes are bad. They are bad because they have a tendency to concentrate upon a firm's weaknesses and lead to surgical operations when what is needed is a concentration and reinforcement of a firm's strengths, with the knife wielded judiciously here and there.

Nevertheless, failures can never be eliminated, otherwise business would be risk-free, and that it certainly is not. From a negative point of view they can be minimised or avoided, but it is far, far more productive to examine the right things the firm does, the successes it has, and to concentrate upon doing more of these. In this book, the technique proposed is subject to the problem of the effect of inflation upon business. A businessman can use any technique he likes, so long as he takes some action. If this book does no more than to cause a manager to adopt four ideas from the check-list of 212 separate profit improvement suggestions at the back of the book, then its purpose will have been achieved. If he uses the full Systematic Approach to Profit Improvement he may generate over 1,000 ideas from within his organisation relevant to his business and, with the full backing of most people in his company, to help in their implementation.

Part 1

MAKING A PROFIT
DURING INFLATION

1

'How Inflation distorts Business.

The general problem

The world has never experienced such a universal increase in inflation as we are experiencing now and it will continue, at perhaps moderating rates, into the foreseeable future. In ten years of relatively modest inflation up to 1973, prices have increased in Holland by 64%, in Britain by 59%, even in Germany, by 34%. America, Canada, Australia, South Africa — all the advanced western economies — are coping now with an increasing rate of inflation which has been accelerated by a shortage in commodities combined with a fear of resource limitation in the future. The energy crisis heads the list of shortages which include wood, minerals, metals, agricultural products, and all the finished goods which are derived from them. (See Figure 1.1).

The arguments about inflation centre on two themes: cost-*push* or demand-*pull.* The cost-push argument stresses the rising costs of materials and labour pushing up prices which in turn increases other costs in a never-ending screw. The demand-pull argument holds that the main force making for persistent inflation arises from the aggregate demand being greater than the economy can satisfy. If money incomes being generated by production are not being balanced by goods and services coming through to the market then rapid price inflation occurs. The classic formula used by governments to control inflation is to apply a credit squeeze of varying intensity upon the domestic economy. The first impact of such monetary shock treatment however, is seldom to ease inflation.

Average annual % increase in consumer prices.

	1960–1970	1970–1973		1960–1970	1970–1973
Europe			*Asia*		
Iceland	11.8	13.5	Korea	14.0	9.9
Spain	6.0	9.9	India	7.2	10.8
Denmark	5.9	8.0	Japan	5.8	9.0
Japan	5.8	9.0	Pakistan	4.1	13.0
Finland	5.0	9.2	Taiwan	2.9	10.9
Ireland	4.8	9.4	Sri Lanka	2.9	7.0
Norway	4.5	6.8	Malaysia	0.6	4.6
Holland	4.2	7.5			
Britain	4.1	8.7	*Africa*		
France	4.0	6.6	South Africa	2.8	7.1
Sweden	4.0	6.8	Morocco	2.7	5.3
Italy	3.9	7.5	Nigeria	2.6	8.6
Austria	3.6	6.3			
Switzerland	3.3	8.3	*Middle East*		
Belgium	3.0	5.8	Israel	5.3	16.6
Germany	2.7	6.1	Egypt	3.7	2.4
Greece	2.1	11.4	Iraq	2.9	3.9
			Iran	1.8	8.3
South America					
Brazil	43.6	18.2			
Chile	26.7	167.7			
Uruguay	24.6	57.9			
Colombia	11.4	16.6			
Peru	9.7	9.3			
Venezuela	1.0	4.0			

Source: The Economist Intelligence Unit March 9, 1974

Figure 1.1   Inflation rates around the world

It creates a crisis in liquidity, followed by crises in production and employment. (See Figure 1.2).

It is clear that rising inflation as a world wide phenomenon is being imported into advanced economies through raw material scarcity. The ability of an individual country to control this kind of inflation through short-term fiscal means is virtually nil. What individual governments are capable of doing by fiscal measures is to further disrupt the process and add to the problems. The increasing rate of inflation makes the problem worse since the trend of the increase also helps to disrupt market demand. The market over-stocks with

Changes in the general index of retail prices	*Percentage change*	*Changes in prices of selected basic materials purchased by manufacturing industry (excluding food, drink and tobacco)*	
	May 1973– May 1974		*May 1973– May 1974*
All items	+16.0	Crude oils	+240.5
Groups		Iron ore	+29.0
Food	+17.2	Aluminium ingots	+37.6
Alcoholic drink	+11.8	Copper	+93.6
Tobacco	+22.6	Zinc	+128.5
Housing	+14.2	Tin	+123.9
Fuel and light	+14.3	Nickel	+11.2
Durable household goods	+14.9	Imported paper and	
Clothing and footwear	+18.4	paperboard	+43.4
Transport and vehicles	+17.9	Imported newsprint	+44.0
Miscellaneous goods	+15.0	Imported softwood	+52.0
Services	+11.2	Hides and skins	11.5
Meals bought and		Raw cotton	+46.3
consumed outside		Imported raw wool	−17.5
the home	+14.4	Natural rubber	+48.0
All items except food	+15.5	Imported woodpulp	+49.9
All items except items of			
food whose prices show		All basic materials	+78.2
significant seasonal			
variations	+16.2		
Items of food, the prices			
of which show			
significant seasonal			
variations	+11.5		

British inflation, 1973/4, Source: Department of Industry and Department of Employment.

Figure 1.2   Inflation: industry costs and consumer prices

goods which are expected to rise in price, thereby increasing the demand-pull effect. There is subsequently a reduction of savings, as enterprises and individuals put their money into tangible and limited assets such as property, land, antiques, and speculate in scarce commodities which are not easily renewed. The effect is to drive governments towards a controlled economy. This means that, through government legislation on prices, wages, profits and interest rates, all classes of society are prevented from earning the income they might otherwise earn. In mixed economies, governments attempt to exert more control through increasing the extent of the public sector, where they have direct access, at the expense of private enterprise.

In the first six months of 1974, no less than fifteen governments in western countries were changed or toppled from power. In one-third of the cases, the extremely rapid rise in inflation due to the world commodity shortage could be seen to be the causative factor, and in twelve of the fifteen cases the elections were fought principally on domestic measures to combat inflation. Inflation also has a distorting effect upon business in all countries, unlike any other. The problem is that a business is never quite sure where it stands. Management believes that it has invested wisely, made a proper provision for future contingencies, protected its resources and provided for a real growth in wealth, only to find its calculations entirely wrong as the value of money is eroded. Companies find themselves unable to meet their commitments, their suppliers in trouble, their markets changed. Supposedly profitable customers go bankrupt and bad credit risks abound. The labour force is disruptive and management morale sinks.

Three factors emerge clearly. The first is that top management must seek a careful route through the labyrinth of pressures even if it means taking a path which the company has never considered before. This may mean making plans based upon a nil growth in output, but with the necessity of surviving profitably and providing for increasing costs which may not be entirely matched by the ability to increase prices. For fast-growth companies, this will call for a radical reappraisal of priorities.

The second factor is that management must not believe that things are well when they are not. For example, the standard techniques for assessing depreciating machinery assume that the new machine will cost no more than the old one. With machine prices rising at 15% per annum and the likelihood that more sophisticated models will be required, the depreciation figures provide nowhere near enough funds for replacement. If corporation tax is levied at a rate of 50% of net profits, then a company must earn profits of four or five times the historic cost of the machinery, just to stay in business. Inflation accounting therefore is a vital necessity at times of escalating inflation. Philips of Eindhoven, the electrical giant, has used a system of 'replacement accounting' for twenty years in order to compare the performance of their overseas branches on a realistic basis. Complacency is very dangerous during inflation. British managements, for example, may be pleased to note that they have 16 companies in the list of Europe's top 20 most profitable firms. But the situation in Britain encourages a company to declare high dividends to shore up its Stock Market rating, whereas the real value of a company's assets may be suddenly inflated by the changing values of its factory sites and other fixed assets. By not reinvesting, many companies are surviving only by allowing their manufacturing capacity to run down and to use outdated equipment.

The third factor is for management to focus the organisation ever more sharply on the need for profit improvement. Without a profit improvement programme a company must rely upon increases in prices and labour productivity or an increase in sales to maintain its wealth. Many of the richer seams for productivity opportunities may be mined out. For other companies, their markets will downturn at worst, remain static at best. Competitive pressure or government interference will restrain their freedom to raise prices fully. In any case, the act of raising prices sows the seeds of the inflation which caused the price increase in the first place. The fiscal problems of world inflation will be eased no doubt. This is likely to be done through governments recognising the need to systematically eliminate the distortions which occur and to introduce gradual reforms, probably allowing costs to be 'indexed' to an expected rate of inflation. (It was in this way that Brazil managed to bring her inflation down from 100% per annum in one quarter ten years ago, to a manageable 15% before the oil crisis in late 1973). With an indexed wages policy now applied in one form or another throughout Europe combined with the use of inflation accounting techniques in the more advanced multi-national companies, the short-term problem will be eased.

The really long term problem remains, however. The world's population is growing, the demands for sophisticated products and services will increase as people become wealthier, but the supply of materials will become more difficult and expensive to procure. The fear of resource limitation and in some cases resource exhaustion in the foreseeable future will grow. The pressures will be on procurement and conservation and not upon sales growth. The buyer will become steadily more important than the salesman. The commodity producers will become more powerful at the expense of the producers of finished goods. As a result, in the next ten years many respectable companies will have become bankrupt, more governments will have fallen and a good deal of social unrest will be experienced.

The shortage of materials

When the oil producers of the Middle East withdrew their supplies from the market, creating the great oil crisis, one of the effects was to escalate immediately the prices they were offered. Another effect was that countries around the North Sea redoubled their efforts to produce oil from the floor of the ocean. The Arab countries knew that national governments were taking more in taxes from the oil than they were paying to the producers. They also realised that there is a limit to the amount of oil they have underground. In twenty to fifty years perhaps, depending upon the view you take of the rate of increase in the use of oil, there will be little left.

By withdrawing oil supplies, the producing countries used a classic method of ensuring a rapid price increase in a fragmented market when there is a limited supply of the goods concentrated in a few hands, with no readily available alternative. They did to oil what Cecil Rhodes did to the diamond in 1889. They stopped selling it. Cecil Rhodes obtained a near monopoly over South African diamond production, calculated that the prices were too low, and immediately agreed to release the output to one customer alone. A buying syndicate was formed; Rhodes pushed the prices up, and finally by 1893 the trade was handled on a fixed percentage basis with an agreement between producers and buyers which has lasted to this day.

As the world demand for scarce resources increases, we can expect more shock tactics like this. In the late 1960's most producers in the oil, chemicals, electricity, natural gas, cement, aluminium, copper, textiles, paper, timber, glass and furniture industries were trying to dispose of surpluses. Their marketing teams were studying market needs, adding customer service, developing new products, with all the trappings of advanced market forcing techniques. In 1973, with accelerating demand added to a three year period of extra warm weather, and with sources beginning to be over-worked, there came the great Year of Shortage. Commodities of all kinds climbed in price, and inflation increased with them. Many companies in these industries, and their customers, are now beginning to practice what has been called 'demarketing'.[1] This can be expected to be almost a permanent feature of life in some industries, enlivened with occasional slumps and booms. The next major shortages are likely to occur in the timber and paper industries, followed by a world shortage in food supply. Materials shortage will continue to exert inflationary pressures, create unemployment and lead to more government interference through price and wage controls, and through allocation systems.

The effect of the shortage will be felt by different companies in a number of different ways. An immediate response to shortage causes a supplying company to make drastic supply cuts to customers. Some companies ration supplies across the board, others are more selective in their choice of customers, basing their judgement on long term goodwill considerations. Where they are free to do so without aggravating government agencies or key customers, they increase their prices. In a period of prolonged shortage they take weak products from the range, reduce advertising and sales costs, and seek to confine their available product to profitable channels with long term potential. Where possible, companies increase their investment in basic research and development to produce substitute materials or to find ways to increase the yield of their existing production. Companies who, as customers, are caught directly in this situation are likely to develop strong purchasing ties with key suppliers, and to carry heavier stocks of critical materials. These companies will also seek to escape from markets which are prone to shortages of raw materials. They will focus their efforts on a profitable set of customers with long term potential. Other companies will hardly be affected, except by the general inflationary pressure. However, even these companies are likely to become more flexible in their operations in case a new situation emerges in their markets, or in their materials supply position. Other companies still, will benefit from the new opportunities which occur. The pressures from consumerists and environmental groups are bound to have an effect upon life styles and hence, purchasing patterns, in some markets. Companies which make products which offer economy with simplicity, and companies with a sound reputation for offering value for money, will benefit from new demand. Market manipulation will be less easy, and emphasis on psychological product differentiation will be lessened. Developing the techniques for building in product obsolescence in an age of shortage when consumerist study teams are gaining more access to information, will be suicidal. Companies making the best use of such changes are likely to carry out more market research, to identify new and changing needs, and to redesign products to suit the quality standards demanded by the markets. It will be difficult for companies to carry out this policy unless there is sufficient profit being generated to cover inflation and to develop the markets. Once again, the need for a profit improvement programme is clear.

Summary of likely effects of inflation and shortage of materials

Such a summary shows:

1   More strain on purchasing departments, as suppliers drop products from their range, increase prices, reduce customer service, and occasionally ration key materials. *Supplier development becomes an important technique.*
2   More strain on research and development departments to install value analysis programmes in order to replace high cost materials with substitutes. *The search for substitutes and synthetics will be widened.*
3   More strain on general management as they meet crises in purchasing, and sharp increases in costs, and as they disinvest in loss making operations.
4   More strain on marketing to provide genuine product and service benefits, identify changes in the markets and concentrate their resources behind profitable long term markets. *Faster reactions to consumer and environmental group pressures will be needed.*
5   More strain on management accounting to provide realistic information about fast changing situations.
6   More strain on production management to provide increases in efficiency, to ease bottlenecks in production and to ensure sound labour relations.

Interference by governments

The effect of rapid inflation and materials scarcity will cause more government interference with business as each country wrestles with the problem of keeping its economy under control. Undoubtedly a good deal of hardship will be caused to people in all kinds of unpredictable ways. Many of the actions which businessmen will feel that they must take in order to survive will be disapproved of by those whose main concern is for social welfare. Similarly, the growing power of consumerists movements, action and protest groups, and political lobbyists will often be backed by legislation. This will inevitably be seen to be directed against business interests, and in many cases the action may be entirely justified. Businessmen in general often confuse those people who oppose business practices with those who are opposed to business principles based as they are upon the capitalist ethos. There are a number of valid arguments against standard business practice which are voiced by intelligent people who have no desire to change the capitalist system. A study of the arguments of opponents can be very revealing. There are certainly some companies which must arrange their policies to suit the wider requirements of society as a whole as well as their markets, their shareholders and their employees.

References

1 P. Kotler, S. Levy, 'Demarketing, yes, demarketing', *Harvard Business Review*, November/December 1971.

2

The Systematic Approach to Profit Improvement

This approach was first used in June 1971. An internationally famous manufacturing company had cut off its Rhodesian subsidiary company several years previously as a result of international sanctions being applied. Officially, no imports and exports were allowed to and from the country. Local companies faced the fact that they must now manufacture for themselves many of the products which they had previously imported, and that they had nowhere to sell them except to the tiny Rhodesian market. This particular company arranged a one-day seminar on the subject of pricing strategy. During the course of the meeting the executives were posed the following question:

> Assume that your company needs an additional 10% net profit, and that government pricing legislation will not allow you to obtain it through a price increase of 10%. What other means are available to you for obtaining the profit?

The thirty-five executives were each asked to list six different ways in which they themselves would approach the problem. They were not required to restrict themselves to their own departmental functions and were set no time limit within which to gain the profit.

The ideas which emerged included the following: reduce the sales force, develop new products, improve labour efficiency, cut the size and vary the quality of some of the products, use cheaper raw materials, increase advertising, cut the advertising, deliver from a central warehouse and shut regional depots and allow shorter credit. In all, 42 separate ideas were produced and recorded for general examination. Each in its own way was relevant and practical, although inevitably many of them would cause dissension and argument. Many of the ideas were in direct conflict with each other. 'Cut the advertising', came from a work study engineer, while 'Increase the advertising' came from a sales executive.

Each of the ideas was then quickly assessed as to: How would it be done, if it were carried out? How much money would it make in a full-going year? How long would it take before the company was earning this money? The audience was asked for their rough and ready guesses on these questions, and the answers from the originators of the ideas were recorded after a short discussion. In the case of the ideas selected above the rough answers were:

Reduce the sales force. This was proposed, strangely enough, by the sales manager. He claimed that since the company had a virtual monopoly in some of its lines, he could afford to reduce the level of sales effort without affecting sales volume. For the same reason he did not much like the idea of his colleague who suggested increasing the advertising budget. Both of them agreed, however, that some restructuring of the sales force was possible, while additional advertising behind the products in competitive markets would be useful. He thought the company could save three men. After providing them with notice, holiday pay and leaving benefits, it would take four months before the full cost saving of 15 000 Rhodesian dollars (£9 000) would begin to be felt in the company figures.

Develop new products. The production manager complained that the company had little research and development resource, and he felt that there was an opportunity to develop some new products, using the existing production equipment. Plant and materials are exceptionally scarce in Rhodesia and the need for conserving them is paramount in everyone's mind. He wanted a development technologist to be hired from South Africa to modify and develop the product range. Although he felt that the profits would not be made in less than 18 months, he expected them to be substantial, producing additional gross profit, after the cost of materials and direct labour of around 1 000 000 Rhodesian dollars (£600 000).

Improve labour efficiency. This was a work study idea, which would need a labour incentive bonus and a cut in absenteeism. The savings might be 10 000 Rhodesian dollars (£6 000) and would take six months to begin to come through.

Reducing the size of products. On products where this was possible, cutting the size would save up to 5% of the material cost. This equated to 50 000 Rhodesian dollars (£30 000), and could be done in three months, after working through the stock in trade and finished goods. The sales people did not like the idea much.

Using cheaper raw materials. This was not found to be practical, however desirable it might seem in theory, simply because the purchasing department could not gain access to cheaper suppliers. The idea was withdrawn without argument.

Changes in advertising. Tampering about with his budget was slightly resented by the publicity manager. He felt he might take a cut of 4 000 Rhodesian dollars (£2 400) with reasonable safety if he had to, and it would take three months before he would save money. The possible sales effect of increases in his budget he found impossible to quantify.

Delivery from a central warehouse. This was a project the company was examining. It was expected to take two months to complete the study, one month to agree the decision, and eight months before the changes were complete. The delivery-service cycle would be lengthened for the rural districts, but the company would save on its revenue budgets and provide more working funds through a reduction in its fixed assets once the properties were sold. The savings might amount to 40 000 Rhodesian dollars (£24 000) a year, and take over eighteen months to be fully effective. Additional savings might be found in production planning, stock control, order processing and sales administration as a result of the study, once an integrated system was introduced.

Allowing shorter credit. The average debtor position was ten weeks, and the financial controller thought this might be reduced to eight weeks, with more pressure on overdue accounts. He thought it would take him about three months to achieve, but when he calculated the savings he found that the cost of financing the extra two weeks of credit was about 14 000 Rhodesian dollars (£6 000) which was a bit less than he had originally reckoned. As he pointed out however, if he lengthened the creditors also, it would improve the cash flow situation considerably.

Price increase. Someone pointed out that even under the price legislation the company could obtain a 3% price increase. Allowing for a slight fall off in sales of the competitive products, this was estimated to produce an additional 100 000 Rhodesian dollars (£60 000) which would start flowing into the company within a matter of six weeks.

From this exercise, which lasted about four hours, the following conclusions were drawn:

1 Nothing acts on a company's profits as quickly as a price increase which does not depress sales.

2   All ideas for profit improvement take hard effort to implement, with the exception of price changes.
3   Profit improvement ideas suitable for rapid introduction produce little extra profit, except from price increases.
4   The biggest profit improvement areas are those where several different departments and functions are involved.
5   All profit improvement ideas, including price changes, involve risk. There is risk to production efficiency, to customer service, risk of a product being unacceptable or a failure risk of material waste, risk of losing supplier goodwill, and so on.
6   Cost saving ideas within the individual departments may cause additional costs in other departments. For example, when credit lines are shortened in the accounts department, the number of customer complaints increase and consequently so do field sales calls on these customers.

When this session ended, the audience were posed the same problem once more by the seminar leader. This time however, they each had to write down the four best ideas which appealed to them out of all those discussed. The results were collated, and sixteen different profit improvement ideas were sent through to senior management for scrutiny. Four projects were started to examine different schemes, three of which were completed successfully. Additionally, six other ideas were built into departmental budgets. Some of them were for increases in expenditure. For example, the production chief got his research and development man, aided by the management accountant who made out the financial case for him. Other budgets were cut. The traceable results of this activity added up to an additional profit in the order of 80 000 Rhodesian dollars (£48 000), by the end of the first year.

Since then the technique has been modified and used in many companies in a variety of industries in several different countries. It has always been successful in directing the attention of managers to the need for continuous profit improvement and in setting out broad lines of direction. It has shown up the nature of the interaction between different departmental functions, and has acted as an important change agent for the start of the profit improvement process.

Standard cost-efficiency techniques

Productivity and cost reduction

All the normal techniques for improving efficiency within a business can be deployed in this approach. The early work of profit improvement involved devising productivity bonus schemes for the labour force. This is still a fundamental technique used by most companies in some degree. As more labour-saving mechanisation is introduced into industry, so trade unions offer their cooperation in return for increased rates of pay for those of the workforce who remain. To introduce productivity bargaining into a highly productive labour situation is sometimes dangerous, since the potential savings often look more attractive than they really are when offset against higher rates of pay. Additionally, a new and potentially disruptive element may have entered into wage bargaining. Similarly, straightforward cost reduction programmes introduced piecemeal into different departments are often treated with hostility by the staff who feel that their budgets, if not their jobs, may be threatened. Straight-line cuts in budgets often have a distorting effect upon the business, however necessary they may be in a financial crisis. A budget cut in one department may easily push up costs in another.

Systematic value analysis

A systematic value analysis programme carried out on the company's products and purchases can reap very handsome rewards in the early stages, but there is a point of diminishing returns. When a long standing product range has not been systematically examined in terms of product formulation, engineering and quality tolerances, and materials used, then a value analysis study will start with those products within the range having the highest potential for cost savings, and gradually move down the list of products until the projects which remain look decidedly risky in terms of cost saving potential. There also comes a point where, to achieve more savings, the product quality itself must be degraded. This is another result of untrammelled inflation. The pressure on costs is always in advance of the company's ability to raise prices. Profit must consequently be maintained from efficiency increases. Once the obvious savings have been taken, then companies are forced to cut the quality of the products they produce and the level of service they provide. To survive in an industry which has been distorted by inflation, will mean producing down to the quality that the law allows. Indeed, some companies may take a chance and go beyond the legal limit. This, in itself, gives rise to consumer disaffection which increases the pressure on governments to tighten up consumer legislation. Such legislation nearly always over-specifies, thereby forcing additional costs on to companies. So the spiral of inflation, leading to higher costs, leading to reduced quality, leading to higher imposed standards, leading to inflation, goes on. Such a spiral is happening in every Western economy in the world, from America to Europe to Australia and South Africa, and will continue for the foreseeable ten years to come.

Profit improvement teams

The technique which is steadily becoming more popular among larger organisations is the setting up of special Profit Improvement Teams. They may be called by various other names such as Cost Improvement Units, but they all involve the establishment of a small team composed of different specialists which then acts as an internal consultancy group. This is pointed at divisional functions or subsidiary units in order to work with operational managers to improve profit performance. Provided with full authority by top management, their task is to combine their own management experience with each operational function in turn, working with the line management during the study, and leaving line management to carry on the tasks. This method can be immensely successful, but its limiting factor is that it can only be applied to strategic sectors of the business one at a time.

The advantages of the systematic approach

All these techniques and others may be needed, once the decision to set up a profit improvement programme has been taken. However, there is one other process which is required as a first step, in order to involve all members of management teams, whether at general management level or through functional departments, down line management, with the aim of generating profit improvement ideas which will be implemented with enthusiasm by managers within their day to day operations. This constitutes a simple technique which has been developed into a Systematic Approach with several advantages.

The approach is simple enough to be used by general management without the need for outside consultants to install it, nor does it call for any alteration to on-going company routines. It can be applied to the business as a whole, and down the line into key areas of the business, or within single departments. It can be used, for example, to review changes in the product mix, or to generate labour efficiency ideas, without involving any other department. The approach has the enormous advantage of using the specialised knowledge and experience of middle and junior management who often see problems and opportunities which remain unobserved by senior management, but in such a way as will not threaten the standing of senior management. It can lead to highly imaginative and creative solutions to problems not considered by operating management. It causes the management team to question ingrained attitudes and practices. It is excellent for resolving short-term crises as well as for shaping the long term directions of the corporate plan. The approach is capable of showing up the interactive nature of the business, in that it can show the effect of decisions taken in one part of the business upon the rest and it can be used as a dynamic process, capable of being continually applied, usually as an early stage of the annual budgeting procedure, so that profit opportunities are systematically reviewed. Finally, the approach acts as a change agent. The people involved in the process understand the objectives and participate in the decision to pursue them. Departmental politics will remain, but it is difficult for individuals to resist the social pressure to conform to decisions taken for the good of a company as a whole. Part 3 of this book details the procedures for implement-ating the Systematic Approach to profit improvement.

The attitude of employees

A straight cost-reduction programme makes staff nervous and often hostile. Yet a profit improvement programme can be shown to meet the specific needs of staff, many of whose jobs might be threatened by inflation. During conditions of rapid inflation, staff need reassurance on three counts:

1   They need to be assured that the purchasing power of their earnings will be maintained by rises which are at least at the level of inflation. Since the company can only pay such increases out of the additional wealth it generates, then at least they can be assured that through a Profit Improvement Scheme, the company is taking steps to create extra wealth in addition to countering inflation of costs.
2   Additionally, staff need to feel secure about their present jobs, and to be provided with an opportunity for career advancement. Clearly, if the company is successful in countering inflation and market distortion through a planned profit improvement programme then their security is assured. A profit improvement programme also opens up opportunities for new developments, for project leaders, for creative ideas, for cooperative staff, and these should all be reflected in the promotional system.
3   Staff need to feel significant within a company and to have a sense of identity. Because this technique calls for the involvement of personnel at various levels, each contributing to decisions which affect their own work and the work of the company as a whole, then to the extent to which each person contributes, he or she is obviously important and significant.

3

Methods of Creating Profit Improvement Ideas

Staff interrelation

The way that managers interrelate is vital to the Systematic Approach to profit improvement.

In any profit improvement activity there are two interdependent aspects. The first is the content of the task being undertaken, the second is the way in which people approach the task. Any group which needs to be effective must work through basic stages. First, the aim or task of the group must be agreed between its members; second, members must exchange ideas and information so that a continuous process of systematic problem solving and decision making takes place, otherwise the group discussions will be wasted. Group members must be capable of developing reasonably harmonious relationships providing mutual support for each other. Irrespective of the task itself therefore, there are also two quite independent basic requirements which must be met first: namely, the group members must be carefully chosen for their skills in social processes and creativity, as much as for their experience and knowledge of the subject; and the environment in which they operate within the company must be supportive and encouraging.

Another important basic factor is that any Profit Improvement Programme will involve change within the organisation, once decisions are being implemented. There are four distinct patterns of organisational response which are necessary to achieve effective change. These are:

1   The acceptance of the role and contribution of the change agent whether it be a profit improvement project team, a systems analyst, or a consultant.
2   The resolution of underlying fears about the change and how it might affect the organisation and individuals.
3   Obtaining identification with, and commitment to specific action so that changes are actually made.
4   Building into the organisation a method of reappraising the changes, and modifying systems structure and management tasks, as required.

The use of the Systematic Approach acts primarily as a change agent at the various levels of the hierarchy. Initially, when executives and managers from interdependent functions within the company are brought together, the situation of the company can be explained, the future projected, and the necessity for a Profit Improvement Programme can be demonstrated. At the same time, the group can be briefed with sufficient data to demonstrate for themselves how sensitive are the company profits to various actions the company can take. Finally, the group could be provided with a 'double bind' question such as being asked for ideas to raise profits by 10% without touching prices, with the purpose of stimulating other suggestions.

This type of meeting is a starter process which invites the participation of management and staff in the overall task. Once projects are determined in detail for implementation, it makes the acceptance of change easier. It may not eliminate entirely any underlying fears staff may have but, because they have participated and have seen the logic for themselves it eases much of their worry. It is also easier to secure commitment to action if the company executives and personnel have been involved from the start and are provided with periodic reviews of the profit improvement results.

When starting a Systematic Approach to profit improvement it is essential for senior management to become involved and to follow the programme through thoroughly. A saving on paper is not a saving until someone has been taken out of the organisation, or a price has been changed, or an item of plant, a depot, a factory site or other piece of land has been sold, some cheaper material has been purchased, or a customer has bought more. Until then, the savings are only paper ones and the balance sheet will look no different.

The success of the approach depends upon the reconciliation of individual needs and goals, among managers at all levels of the hierarchy, recognising that some will be threatened by it, some will be promoted through it, and that all may feel uneasy while it is going on.

As a result there must be coordination between functions and cooperation between executives. There is a stronger need for feedback up the organisation than for communication down the line. Managers know where greater efficiency could be achieved but they need senior management to provide them with the specific aims and the motivation to achieve them. Furthermore, managers will be the ones who will have the task of operating new systems under a changed organisation. Whether they are effective or not will depend upon how much they have participated in the decision to change and how sensitive senior management is to the human problems involved in activating the change.

The project team

In recruiting the members of a project team to study problems and evaluate solutions there are certain necessary requirements: the group should consist of members not separated too far from each other in the hierarchy. They should be able to respect each other without too much deference to age, seniority or experience. The members need to be sufficiently flexible, and reasonably open in their approach to problems so that they can ask for a change of brief if they find their task too narrowly defined, and can devise unusual solutions. The group must combine differences in experience and function. The size norm seems to be more than four and less than nine. Finally, the group should be able to consider its task without being inhibited by an authoritarian leader, but also have sufficient direction to prevent discursiveness through lack of motivation.

Membership of a successful profit improvement project team will have an effect upon its members which should be recognised for management development purposes: they will be seen to be contributing effectively and creatively to the accomplishment of worthwhile objectives. They will be exercising more initiative, responsibility and creativity than their normal jobs allow. They will develop their skills in social control and social processes and may find ways to tap the creative abilities of their subordinates. Their overall capacity for problem analysis and assessment will improve, as will their decision making ability.

Project methodology

The Coverdale Technique for problem solving in groups is probably the best of the standard approaches. This requires that groups proceed through the following stages:

1   Define the aim and purpose of the group. This is a much more difficult stage than appears at first sight. Time spent on accurately defining the aim will be more than worthwhile in terms of the quality of results. Reflective thinking is most useful at this stage; it is often irritating to the more energetic problem solvers in the group but it must be recognised as a distinct skill of a high order. If someone does no more than to project the right scope and aim for the group, widening aims which are too narrow by asking 'Why?', and

narrowing aims which are too wide by asking 'How?', he will have made a major contribution to the group result.

2   Gather and record relevant knowledge, experience, evidence and ideas. This is also a stage which must be considered at length, and again irritates the energetic members of a group, who can be most harmful by their desire to push on to a conclusion and by their general inability to listen to what is being discussed. The quieter and more reflective personalities are again most productive at this stage. The recording procedure is important for a successful 'holistic' approach, ie making certain that every angle has been covered. The use of a visual aid to record pieces of information submitted by the group is very important.

3   Plan what has to be done, by whom, when, and how. This is where the men of action come into their own. Having a tendency to scan problems for an immediately visible solution they can now determine better than most the action which must be taken, and how.

For an open-ended problem, requiring the evaluation of many possible solutions over a period of time, the Coverdale Technique requires that the first three stages, of aim-setting, information-gathering, and action determination be repeated many times. In this way the total body of information and knowledge grows, uncertainties are gradually reduced to known factors, and the problem as a whole can be worked through to the optimum solution. The two final stages in the process are:

4   Carry out the action.
5   Review the process and analyse the results.

The final stage, (5) is very important as a learning process for the whole of the group. It should review the way in which the group arrived at a final decision, making an analysis of how the decision was arrived at and how effective it was. In this way, their performance will improve subsequently and they will begin to perceive the social process skills of others while identifying their own strengths and weaknesses.

Thinking processes

Creativity as a concept is not very helpful in determining which particular people should make up a group. 'Creativity' is defined as the ability to produce original ideas, or new solutions to problems. Novelty is one aspect of creativity but only insofar as it may be relevant to the problem. Another is transformation, the re-arrangement of old ideas into something new. Yet another is condensation, which means that the truly creative idea is one which does not necessarily divulge all its impact with the first impression, whereas non-creative ideas are soon squeezed dry of meaning.

Intelligence does not appear to be strongly associated with creativity, within the intelligence tolerances set by most management tasks. Age appears to be quite an important factor. Studies show that the years of most creative production are under 30 for chemistry and poetry, 30–34 for mathematics, physics, botany, symphonies, 35–39 for astronomy, physiology, opera and philosophy, and over 40 for novels and architecture.[1] Other studies show that over 50% of the total output of creative ideas are produced by less than 10% of the population. The problem for profit improvement teams is to recognise who these people might be. What is probably more important than a search for high creativity however, is the easier task of identifying the different types of thinking which people use in their approach to problems, and to ensure an appropriate mix of styles.

In the past six years, there has been a considerable advance in our knowledge of the way people approach problems, largely owing to the work of educational psychologists and those responsible for developing programmed learning techniques. One of the most significant discoveries is that of a distinction between 'convergent' and 'divergent' thinking. The convergent thinker works very hard to obtain results from narrow problems with single solutions while the divergent thinker performs better on open problems where many solutions are possible. It is tempting, though inaccurate, to view the divergent thinker as 'creative' because his free interpretation of problems appears to be more productive of novel ideas. This is not the case; original work comes from convergers and divergers alike. The roots of originality are more likely to lie in personality and not in the way an individual thinks.

The divergent thinker is very useful at the beginning of a problem analysis and in providing stimulus for ideas from a wide range of interests. The converger however, is particularly useful for his diligence in tackling a problem and for following through a line of thinking to the last detail. Divergers differ from convergers in that they are more likely to be liberal and tolerant in their outlook, likely to be emotional, and will probably be humorous. They are less authoritarian, and less likely to change their ground under pressure from opinions of others. Convergers are more than twice as likely to be academically successful than divergers. These are not mutually exclusive types, around 40% of the population can be expected to be balanced between the two, being partly convergent and part divergent.

Within any group there is a need to focus upon all aspects of the subject at first, and then narrow down the field of choice into workable solutions. This provides a serious problem for the style of thinking known as 'scanning'. Here, one possible solution is identified early on and is then pursued until it is found to be impractical, whereupon another solution is selected. An energetic 'scanner' is anathema to effective group working since he has a tendency to push the group to an early and fairly obvious solution, which is probably the most common fault in project work. The scanner may be a very effective executive in his own right, and could be used as an individual to assist in motivating managers to action. But his skills are not analytical, and if he is to be used in a team it should be after the alternative solutions have been considered and evaluated.

Creative stimulus

Some form of artificial 'idea stimulus' can be very effective in unfreezing people's minds to produce original solutions to problems. First however, the barriers to creative thinking must be broken down. These are: a lack of information and knowledge combined with standard routine approaches; an authoritarian group or organisation; a premature evaluation of ideas; rigid attitudes, wrong method of operation and low morale; lack of drive and motivation.

The least obvious, but one of the most important of these is the premature evaluation of ideas. It is more usual to compliment a man in business for his unerring judgement than for having a soaring imagination. The educational system teaches us to be expert critics and evaluators. Nonetheless, when men feel that their ideas are being evaluated on the spot they tend to be more inhibited and self critical. Immediate judgement of ideas has one immediate effect, it blocks the flow of ideas. Any kind of constraint at the idea-producing stage will inhibit the process. Certainly, ideas must be put through evaluation and screening systems at some stage, but not at the moment when they are being produced. One of the most successful profit improvement teams meets to discuss a problem and to produce ideas in the evening. Then the team members go to bed; when they meet the next morning they can begin to evaluate the ideas they were discussing the evening before. The scheme works; the break between idea generation and idea evaluation is vital.

Attribute listing

This technique was developed in the University of Nebraska, and involves listing all the attributes of an object and then modifying different attributes in order to find a new combination that will improve the object. For example, to devise a better mousetrap than the wooden block with a metal spring should not be too difficult. Replace the wood with plastic, improve upon the wire device for killing the mouse and enclose it all together in one piece with a lid. Press a spring on top to release the dead mouse and the mousetrap is perfect. It is clean, noiseless, hygienic, cheap, simple, and safe to operate. As a matter of fact it was developed and manufactured but was one of the biggest new product flops in history. Women were afraid of it, and afraid of the dead mouse, so they did not want to drop it out and the new mousetrap looked too expensive to throw away. It wasn't but it looked as if it was. So the product failed, despite the fact that the world is supposed to beat a path to your door if you can make a better mousetrap, according to the old saying.

Forced relationships

This technique relies upon listing a lot of ideas and then considering each one in relation to every other one as a means of stimulating the idea production process. For example, a manufacturer of office equipment might list separate items he manufactures such as a desk, bookcase, filing cabinet and chair. This may lead him to designing a cabinet with a built-in bookcase. Considering the desk and the filing cabinet he gets the idea of replacing two desk drawers by a filing cabinet drawer. He could go systematically through all the combinations, adding the occasional bizarre item to the list to stimulate the imagination.

Morphological analysis

This is a technique involving structural analysis. The method consists of singling out all the most important dimensions of a problem, and then examining all the relationships between them. If the problem posed is 'getting somewhere from one place to another via a powered vehicle', then one part of the problem is the type of vehicle to use (cart, chair, sling, bed, etc.). Another part of the problem is the medium through which the vehicle operates (air, water, oil, hard surface, rollers, rails, etc.). Another problem is the power source (compressed air, electric motor, steam, moving cables, moving belt, atomic power). If these three dimensions were to describe the problem completely, then the imagination could be stimulated by putting the various combinations together, for example, a cart-type vehicle, powered by an internal combustion engine, moving over hard surfaces, is the familiar car. Some of the combinations will be nonsense, but some may turn out to be novel and provide just the inspiration needed.[2]

Check lists

Although check lists are normally used as a screening device to evaluate answers, they can often be used to provide ideas in other fields of activity. For example, a good check list about how to overcome weaknesses in production can provide inspiration for research and development ideas.

Brainstorming

The previous ideas for stimulating creativity work best with individuals or with small groups. The most popular technique for stimulating creativity among large groups is that of brainstorming. This is a conference for the sole purpose of creating a lot of ideas. Group size should be between six and ten – there should not be too many experts – the problem should be as specific as possible – the session should last about an hour and there should be no more than one problem. The rules are:

1   No criticism allowed.
2   No immediate evaluation of the ideas.
3   What is wanted is; quantity of ideas, combinations of ideas, and developments of ideas.

There has been criticism from industrial and educational psychologists that the quality of the ideas produced at brain-storming sessions is very poor and seldom leads to very sound results.

Synectics

This is a refinement of the brainstorming technique which requires about three hours to complete, and obviates some of the trivialities produced by the brainstorming method. Instead of defining the problem tightly, the leader provides an open brief, initially searching for viewpoints and attitudes rather than for solutions to the problem. In this way the problem takes on a life of its own as the leader gradually injects facts and information so refining the problem down and providing the group with aspects to discuss. Only when the leader senses that the group is near to reaching a good solution to the general problem, will the actual problem be defined. At that point the group will begin to refine the solution. To turn the idea into a reality, further conferences will be held, added to consultation and experimentation. From this technique, sometimes called 'operational creativity' complete answers to difficult problems can be found, rather than piecemeal solutions.

Determining the profit improvement style

One of the key factors in initiating profit improvement projects is to determine beforehand whether the company is going to use a general or 'holist' approach, by taking all the features of the company situation first and then determining priorities for project teams, or whether they will use specific or 'serialist' approach, taking one part of the company's operations at a time and dealing with that thoroughly before moving on to the next. The holist approach corresponds to a certain type of thinking, but implementation across the company needs an examination at the top of the business first. After this a number of priority areas can be selected for profit improvements projects. These latter will require work by several teams to reach implementation.

On the other hand, a serialist approach can be used by setting up one profit improvement team, more or less on a permanent basis, to work through each operational function in turn. In the course of their work the team will act as internal consultants, making heavy use of check lists and management audits, securing the assistance of operating staff and supervisors to implement changes. Often, a member of the team will be left behind when the team moves on, and become a permanent member of the operating function who will see that the proposals are carried through effectively.

References

1   H. C. Lehman, *Age and Achievement*, Princeton University Press, 1953.
2   J. E. Arnold, *Useful Creative Techniques*, Parnes & Harding, 1964.

4

Where to Look for Profit Improvements

There are only three ways to improve profits in any business. Increase sales volume; reduce costs, or alter prices so as to obtain a higher gross margin.

Managers often use more sophisticated terms than these. Altering the gross profits mix of the product range, changing the sales mix, the marketing mix or the customer mix, each of these are routes to the simple objectives of cutting overall costs, raising sales volume, or juggling with prices.

Most companies require only marginal changes in any of these three dimensions to obtain substantial increases in profits (See Figure 4.1). Equally they require only marginal pressures on their sales, costs or prices to make substantial losses. The pressure on prices in a very competitive market is often in the form of providing additional discounts to customers in order to win business.

Assume that the company has the following costs structure: Sales = 100; variable costs of material and direct labour = 50; overhead and marketing costs = 40; net profit = 10.

The objective is to secure an increase in net profit of 50%, quite substantial by any account.

To achieve this it will take only a 10% increase in sales volume (assuming that no more overheads are incurred in handling the extra volume). Or it will take a 12½% reduction in overhead costs to achieve the same end. Or it will take a 10% reduction in variable costs (assuming that product quality is not affected). Or it will take a mere 5% increase in price (assuming no loss of sales volume).

The simple chart in Figure 4.1 is very important for the understanding of the dynamics of volume, costs and profits. A company with a high gross margin and low material cost, say in the drug industry, with a heavy investment in research

To increase profit by 50%:

			or	or
Original		*Raise*	*Cut*	*Raise*
cost		*sales*	*overheads*	*prices*
structure		*by 10%*	*by 12½%*	*by 5%*
100	Sales	110	100	105
50	Variable costs	55	50	50
40	Overhead costs	40	35	40
10	Net profit	15	15	15

Figure 4.1   Example showing a substantial profit increase from changes in sales, overheads or prices

and development, will be much more sensitive to a reduction in overhead costs, or an increase in sales, than will a company with a very high material cost. The latter will obviously be sensitive to a cut in these material costs. There are more of these examples shown in the chapter on management accounting. (Chapter 7).

In any costing exercise it is clear that a change in price has an overwhelming impact upon net profit returns provided that the sales volume does not drop also. Clearly if the company is trading at a high rate of net profit, then the impact of any changes upon costs, sales or prices is proportionately smaller. These changes are correspondingly greater wherever the net profit return is small.

A further point about price changes is that the administrative burden of making a price change is far less than the effect of any decision to cut costs or increase sales volume. The cutting of costs may require a long and detailed study of the business efficiency of the operation and consequently a complex set of decisions will have to be taken. The same problem applies to building an increase in sales. The marketing and selling operation must be extended, again a complex operation involving several levels of management, this time with the added risk that the additional sales volume may not be achieved even with extra effort. Finally, a change in pricing structure achieves a faster return than any other method. To implement a price increase means that additional profit is returning to the company within a matter of weeks, assuming that sales do not fall off. But increasing sales takes a long time for most companies. There may be additional selling expenses to offset against any increased returns. Even if the simplest and quickest methods of cost cutting are used, say firing staff, there will be notice periods to be worked out or paid off, holiday money due, and redundancy payments to meet.

There is a risk attendant in all three circumstances of increasing sales, cutting costs or raising prices. There is a risk that an increased sales effort may be bought at high expense, for example, by increasing discounts or by pushing into unknown markets, or by adding extra promotion costs. There is a risk to product quality, or to management effectiveness in any cost cutting programme. Equally there is a risk in making price changes even when price regulations allow it. This risk operates at two levels. First, sales may be lost to competitive markets. Second, the cumulative effect of all suppliers in an industry making price increases may be to price the product out of the market altogether, making some customers at the margin of demand seek alternative substitute products. One way of improving profits in a company is to search out and buy alternative cheaper materials with a guaranteed supply. The supplier who continually increases his price, even if it is done in concert with his competitors within the industry, will force his customers to look for savings in his product. Finally, there is the overall effect of businesses everywhere seeking to counter inflation by only making price changes which themselves boost the inflationary effect. There is a circular logic in the process, which has a direct impact upon the economy as a whole.

Inflation cannot be countered by prices which drift upwards with it. To lower the rate of inflation, the rate of increase in price levels must be reduced at some point below the rate of increase of costs. That is why profit improvement programmes are so vital during inflationary periods. Profits must be maintained, yet the full effect of cost inflation cannot be passed on, so that something must be done in the areas of cost reductions or sales increases.

The effect of cumulative improvements

On the other hand, so little often needs to be done to increase profits. So far, we have considered costs, sales and prices independently of each other. But if very small improvements are made in each of these areas at the same time, the cumulative impact of such improvements upon the profit return is enormous. If the company is making net profits at the rate of 10% then it can improve on this by nearly a quarter depending upon its costs structure, even if it can only obtain a 1% increase in sales followed by a 1% cut in costs and a 1% lift in price.

If the original company shown in Figure 4.1 were to make tiny changes in prices, sales and costs — changes so small it would be hardly worth bothering to budget for them, the effect upon profits would be dramatic.

If they raise sales by 1%; further reduce overall costs by 1% and lift their price by 1%, they would achieve nearly 25% additional profit.

This does assume that costs remain standard while these changes are going on. Nevertheless the principle can be used in an inflationary period if management sets out a corporate plan based on the objective of a series of planned price increases which will do no more than to counter the estimated cost inflation over the period of the plan. After that, extra pressure might be placed on sales and on costs in order to obtain the required additional net profit objective. It

	The original costs structure	With a 1% sales increase	Followed by a 1% cut in total costs	Followed by a rise in price of 1%
Sales	100	101	101	102
Variable costs	50	50.5	89.55	89.55
Overhead costs	40	40		
Net profit	10	10.5	11.45	12.45

Their net profit goes up by 24.5% on the original.

Figure 4.2   **The effect on profits of a small, combined improvement in sales, costs and prices**

might also be possible to increase the net selling price beyond the inflation of costs by making planned reductions in the discounts offered to new customers on new lines which are outside the scope of most pricing regulations.

None of these actions are risk free. To enforce reductions in discount levels even within pricing regulations for example, can be a difficult exercise, sometimes even more so than making alterations to the basic price list. It is a peculiar phenomenon in marketing that customers usually regard their discounts as being personal to them and a sign of the importance of their relationship to the supplier. The performance of the buying department may even be measured in some companies by their ability to secure an additional discount from the supplier. Such buyers will jealously guard their discounts, while feeling unable to do anything about a price increase which affects all the other customers also. Nonetheless, the discount structure may be changed to the suppliers advantage by his showing the customer how to reduce his purchasing costs. Many customers order too frequently, order the wrong product for their requirement and some require rush deliveries. If an alternative service is supplied which has advantages for the customer as well as for the supplier, then the discount problem may be overcome because both the customer and the supplier make savings. This is where profit improvement technique comes into play. Projects like this just need thinking through in detail. Most salesmen for example, cannot see how an altered delivery arrangement to a particular customer can save money in real terms. The saving may be only tiny when one customer is considered, but grossed up across the entire customer population and across all deliveries the savings may be considerable. Only a management accountant may be able to calculate the amount. The means to such a saving can be found only by a team involving the management accountant, the distribution manager and the sales manager working with each other. The effect of a successful profit improvement project of this kind will be either to reduce the company's discount bill, through providing service which represents a cost saving to the customer, or to lower the company's distribution costs. Surprisingly enough, a company can often achieve both aims after a project team has completed its work. A good project team will find distribution savings and, at the same time, raise the level of service.

Lines of approach to profit improvement

The Systematic Approach to profit improvement calls for the examination of the efficiency of the business in the following order:

1 The interactive savings between functions.
2 The operational savings within functions.
3 The marginal opportunities.

It must start with the highest level of the management hierarchy, and move down the line. Profit improvement projects are classified as to high risk and low risk, and as long-term, medium-term and short-term prospects.

Interactive savings

The most substantial profits can be earned from examination of the interaction of the different functions of the business. In seeking to maximise its own objective, each department costs the others something. The highest rewards will emerge from an examination of the interplay between the different functions, known as the 'interactive effect'. This area is also the source of conflict between functions in a business. Inefficiency arising from this conflict must be tackled first, and because the source of company politics and rivalries is the same area, this requires the active involvement of top management. To see this in operation, take the nature of the objective of each function. Each functional objective is distinct from the objective of other functions, indeed, an objective in one department may be opposed to the objective maintained by another.

For example, it is a characteristic of sales managements that they desire to maximise sales revenue. Given unlimited power to direct matters, they will call for wide area expansion, new product varieties to suit various pockets of demand, and for freedom to negotiate prices and discounts so as to meet competition. They require a high level of delivery service, and reasonably generous credit terms for their customers. (See Figure 4.3 p. 35). This costs other functions a great deal. The production functions prefer few products produced upon highly mechanised lines with an even rate of output so as to enable them to maximise their productivity. They want the right materials on call, at the right time in the right place, negotiating freedom to buy the staff they need, and they want the product shipped out of their stores as soon as it is made. They want to conserve space and labour. Disruption of any kind costs them dear, particularly rush orders or seasonal demand.

The purchasing department wants to buy the best deals it can obtain. With a wide tolerance in the product specification, they can experiment with different suppliers, make special purchases of lower grade materials. They also want a product line composed of fewer different materials and less erratic production offtake. They want ready access to storage space and flexible transport readily available. They can cause trouble to production, quality control, to sales, and to transport and distribution.

The distribution department has one of the most aggravating problems in the business. They are not responsible for the main costs of the business, and are only indirectly influential upon sales volume. In the face of competing and diametrically opposed demands made upon them by sales on one hand and production on the other, they must handle a most complex set of inter-dependent operations at 'least cost'. If they listened to sales demands, they would supply a daily customer service, plus an on-call service for rush orders, and would store the finished goods in many warehouses located close to the markets. If they listened to production demands, they would constantly move products out of the factory and into central warehousing in small volume, and constantly supply a variety of materials in small quantities just when needed.

At the same time the management accountant has set up a budget to restrain them on their materials-handling labour costs, their transport costs, the size and location of their premises, and provided them with a minimum of equipment.

The financial accountant wants fewer customers, cash payments or money in advance if possible, long lines of credit from suppliers, fewer staff everywhere, less equipment and a much reduced capital base for the enterprise, together with a higher rate of profit.

All of this is obviously overstated, but it serves to underline the natural conflicts which occur in business and are necessary for the cost efficient running of an enterprise. Business plans are the result of compromises between functions. Profits are often a measure of the success of the company in handling the conflicts between these interactive objectives. For this reason the profit improvement plan must start with these interactive functions.

The nature of interactive costs is disguised by an annual budgeting procedure, by tradition and by experience. Once an expense budget has been set up inside a company it tends to be continued using the original model of costs but just extending them in scope and in scale. Certainly the annual sales forecast will provide a focus for all the efforts of the different departments in terms of volume and revenue, while the profit objective will provide a focus for costs. But the way in which all these departments operate together is seldom examined. Each year each department requires more of something and less of something else dependent upon the sales and profit requirement. But until a company hits a crisis there is seldom any rational question about the nature and need for the department itself. The longer a company has been in business, the more experience its managers have, and the less likely they are to question the way in

	Other Departments' Requirements:	*Marketing and Sales Requirements:*
Engineering	Long design lead time	Short design lead time
	Functional features	Sales features
	Few models	Many models
	Standard components	Custom components
Purchasing	Standard parts	Nonstandard parts
	Price of material	Quality of material
	Economical lot sizes	Large lot sizes to avoid out of stock
	Purchasing at infrequent intervals	Immediate purchasing for customer needs
Production	Long production lead time	Short production lead time
	Long runs with few models	Short runs with many models
	No model changes	Frequent model changes
	Standard orders	Custom orders
	Ease of assembly	Aesthetic appearance
	Average quality control	Tight quality control
Warehousing	Fast moving items, narrow product line	Broad product line
	Economical levels of stock	Large levels of stock
Finance	Strict rationale for spending	Intuitive arguments for spending
	Hard and fast budgets	Flexible budgets to meet changing needs
	Pricing to cover costs	Pricing to further market development
Accounting	Standard transactions	Special terms and discounts
	Few reports	Many reports
Credit	Full financial disclosures by customers	Minimum credit examination of customers
	Low credit risks	Medium credit risks
	Tough credit terms	Easy credit terms
	Tough collection procedures	Easy collection procedures

Figure 4.3   **How one department's requirements may conflict with other department's**

which it works. Senior management in a company usually recognise this but they realise that it requires a considerable upheaval to even question the matter, let alone do something about it. Questioning the role of an individual department is a big enough job for senior management, for the departmental team themselves to do it is an impossible task.

The fundamental question

One of the ways to start examining interactive costs is to reduce the company and its operation to a theoretically very small size with very limited resources. For example, the question could be asked: 'If this company was being set up again from scratch in this industry, financed by limited funds, what are the essential operations it would require'. This is a fundamental question which it is extremely useful to ask when examining the rationale behind any activity and evaluating its importance. Purchasing, production, distribution and sales come high on the list of essential functions, with corporate planners, personnel management and other staff services fairly low. The question does not eliminate them from the company, but it does position their function within an order of importance.

The same question can be asked within each department. 'If we had to start this department all over again, from a very small base, what would we require first and what last?' Most profit improvement programmes start with what is being done at present and try to examine how it could be done better indeed, this theme will be found throughout this book. But at the formulation stage of any profit improvement project it can be most revealing to examine the subject from an entirely different angle. Having decided on the work to be done, assume ideal conditions for doing it, produce an ideal interactive system within which the various functions could work together. From here, the technique is to develop a working system by introducing the minimum modifications required for this ideal system to carry out the work, despite divergences from ideal conditions. The theory holds that it is better to work to an ideal model of how the work should be done, rather than build step by step on an existing organisational model which may be out of date and is far from ideal.

Reorganisation

Most company organisations are years out of date. The worst effects may have been removed by organisational changes, but usually the structure is based on conditions which no longer exist. Most businesses today are radically different from the businesses they were ten years ago. They operate in new markets with new products, in different geographical areas, with new manufacturing techniques and with more sophisticated equipment. Yet their organisational structures usually remain similar to the structures existing ten years before with the addition of a few new services at management level and perhaps a reorganisation of the sales force structure.

In this book the argument is, that owing to inflation and creeping shortages of key materials, most businesses will be undertaking radically different activities in ten years' time, from the work they are doing today. Many of them will require in addition radical reshaping. One of the most consistent effects of a successful takeover bid is that the purchaser usually clears out a lot of the old systems, the old products, and many of the existing managers. The company upon whom these wounds are inflicted believes them to be mortal, that the company will never be the same again, 'it will never be successful like this,' they say. Yet they often take a loss in the first year but find by the second that profits are flowing through the organisation once more, morale has returned and a new spirit has infected the company.

Difficult though it may be for a management team to carry out such surgery upon itself, for some companies, in the difficult trading conditions of the next ten years, the operation will be vital. Reorganisation will come in some form or another, either at the hands of the existing management or at the hands of some new owner. Reorganisation is clearly a subject which only top management can handle. No manager will willingly commit hari-kiri upon himself and his colleagues.

Departmental trade-offs

The interactive costs between departments can be improved lower down the hierarchy between managers from different functions. Three principles should be followed to find economies down the line. The first is that the project team must consist of managers who cover the functions which interact together, the second, that the information relating to the costs and profit opportunities in each function must be made available to each member of the team, the third is that the team must be put under pressure to produce profits together as a team. The pressure to obtain results must be intense enough to cause each manager to produce 'trade-offs' between his own function and others. A 'trade-off' is where one manager agrees to sacrifice some requirement from another department in order to exchange it for a saving in his own operation. A purchasing officer may agree to put a quality control man on his own budget to check incoming goods, lifting the responsibility from production in exchange for the right to make occasional low cost purchases of sub-standard goods which might increase factory wastage.

A useful device is for senior managers to ask the project team to produce merely a list of opportunities, not a list of decisions or recommendations. In this way, the team of middle managers is not asked to decide anything, the decision is left to their superiors after they have considered the results. This removes the human problems of deciding about their colleagues' and subordinates' future, from the managers concerned.

The four basic principles

Within each operational function the Systematic Approach to profit improvement demands that four basic principles be followed: first, the maximum
savings are to be found by eliminating an operation entirely, without throwing
the burden on to another department. If an operation can be removed, rather
than modified or improved, the feasibility of doing so should be examined first.
Second, in theory, any item of expenditure should contribute its full share of
overhead and net profit contribution. It is not sufficient for a value analysis
programme merely to save its own cost of operation, or for a new purchasing
system to save its own direct cost of salaries and expenses. Some items of
management expense are very difficult to quantify in this way, from the
managing director's car to the advertising programme, but the principle is
unarguable and should be followed even if management judgement on a
subjective basis is used for the assessment. The marginal items of expenditure,
where there is considerable doubt about their payoff may be continued in the
business and used as a kind of contingency fund, being the first things to go in a
time of crisis. Such marginal items of expenditure may be of very small
consequence, but added together the total of these self indulgences, for that is
what they are, may be considerable. The third principle to be followed is that
however perfect a system appears, there is no reason to believe that something
better does not exist. If an operation is already highly efficient then it should
still be examined for three reasons:

1   The price of the operation's efficiency could be a heavy cost burden to
    another function.
2   There may be lessons to be learnt from its operation, or in its development,
    which could be applied elsewhere in the business.
3   It might not be seen to be so efficient if another management accountant
    costs it.

The fourth principle is never to assume that any item of cost is necessary, and to
take nothing for granted. A cost is cleared only after it is shown to have
produced worthwhile results; until then it is suspect and subject to appraisal.

Marginal costs and opportunities

Finally, the examination of a business for profit improvement calls for an
examination of the marginal opportunities in each function. When the
Systematic Approach is used, a group of managers is asked to nominate those
activities under their control which would have to be dispensed with, should
there be a budget cut across the board of, say, 10%. They can be reassured that
their company is not necessarily intending to make such a cut, but merely wants
them to examine the question and to produce a list of operations which would

have to be cut out, together with an assessment of the risk involved, and the work which would be required to obtain the savings.

At the same time the sales department should produce a list of 'marginal' sales opportunities which, though small, might be obtained from a very limited expansion of their resources. These additional sales opportunities might be counted in the form of new territories to be exploited, new small markets, or in the form of modified products. At the same time, marketing and sales personnel should be asked to list those products or services which could stand a price increase without threatening sales volume, and to indicate those accounts where a discount could be reduced in coordination with an alteration of service. The purpose of these lists is to show management the operations which are considered as of marginal value by the managers. The test of assessing each item of expenditure, in terms of its own full contribution to overheads and net profit, can then be applied. Senior management can weigh the risks attached to any saving and apply a contingency reserve to the central budget. In this way, if an expenditure item is cut it can be replaced if it is seen that the operation is being damaged in the process. The effect of producing a list of marginal opportunities is threefold. First, it concentrates the attention of managers on the need for cost-effectiveness within their operations and they tend to apply sterner tests of profitability to future expenditure. Second, it leaves their superiors with the decision as to which items to eliminate. Third, it provides management with another hedge against a crisis. Even if senior management does not accept the possible savings suggested by a manager, if a crisis comes they can judge how much possible profit margin there may be within the organisation which can be explored if they so decide. Usually these lists indicate features of the operation which are designed with a long-term view and senior management have the task of weighing up the balance between the need for profits now against the need for security and growth tomorrow.

Main profit making opportunities

1   The biggest improvement in profits will come from examining changes needed simultaneously in sales, costs, and prices, and in particular, from examining the nature of interactive costs between departmental functions.
2   The largest profit opportunities will be obtained only in the long term, and may require a great deal of effort. The development for the first time of new products, within a company having a static product line, is a good example.
3   It is important to attack the strategic areas of the business ie those in which 80% of the results are obtained from 20% of the activity.
4   It is important to examine long standing practices systematically as well as organisation structures, and those high cost operations which are considered to be efficient.
5   The generation of extra profit today may involve some risk to the future. Many of the immediate cost savings will be made on projects with a long

payoff. A profit improvement programme calls for a judgement by senior management as to the question of balancing the interest of profit, security, and growth.

6   Short-term profit improvements are usually those linked to surgery on the organisation or changing prices. However, the use of a long-term profit improvement approach throws up a number of such opportunities automatically, and these can be held in a contingency reserve against a downturn in the market.

Part 2

INFLATION AND BUSINESS OPERATIONS

5

Profit Improvement in General Management

'How would you improve the effectiveness of the organisation while at the same time making a 10% cut in overhead costs?' Executives, faced with this question, and with the task of increasing both effectiveness and cost reduction, can use it as a basis on which to examine both general management activity and the management structure of a particular functional division. The question needs simple modification to suit the particular circumstances of a company. For example, to direct the attention to the long term, a series of time scales can be added to the cut in costs – for example '. . . a 10% cut in overheads this year, and a 20% cut by year three.'

Two points should be repeated about these double bind questions. First, they are artificial questions, not to be regarded as company policy at this stage, but designed to provoke new thinking about the way the business is run. Second, the executives involved should not take inflation into account with their ideas, but take business costs as they are at present. The calculations for inflation recovery can be made subsequently, once the profit improvement projects are selected – although the expected cost of inflation is implicit in setting up the objective in the question. In other words, if inflation is expected at the rate of 10% over the following year, then the projects selected to meet the objective will enable the company to maintain its present profit position, assuming that it does not raise prices. In practice, a company will have to raise its prices during inflation. This is necessary because few profit improvement projects will be able to save the full cost of inflation in any one year without heavy surgery on the company organisation. Most profit improvement projects of consequence take two and sometimes three years to pay off by which time inflation may have climbed by 35% or more.

Improving the profitability of general management requires a study of five main areas:

1   Salaries and indirect wages.
2   Running expenses.
3   Fixed costs.
4   Organisation structure.
5   Management system and routine.

These five areas are all interactive and interdependent. It will pay first to examine organisation structures and management systems because this is where the most significant improvements can be found.

Organisation structures

The ten key questions

In examining any activity or expense the following questions need to be asked:

1   Can it be eliminated without much harm to the results?
2   Does it cost more than it is worth?
3   Can it be reduced in scope and cost?
4   Does it do more than is required?
5   Can it be done more cheaply another way?
6   Can it be done more cheaply by someone else?
7   Is there an alternative service from outside which is adequate but cheaper?
8   Can the services or expenses supporting the operation be reduced?
9   On a management judgement basis can the operation be sensibly considered to provide its full share of overhead and net profit contribution?
10   How does it affect other costs in the business?
11   If you were to start the business again, would you include it?

Organisational weaknesses

The primary causes of organisational weaknesses are; *a* vague reporting relationships which mean that staff are unclear as to whom they report and who reports to them. It is a common feature in smaller businesses to find one man reporting to two superiors. *b* an organisational pattern which was originally based upon the circumstances of a business which has now substantially changed; *c* an unplanned organisation which has developed without reference to the organisational requirements of each function or of the need for integration; *d* duplication of functions and conflict between functions; *e* managers with too many staff reporting to them or managers with excessive personal workloads; *f* a lack of delegation of authority; *g* the absence of clearly defined objectives; *h* failure to assign responsibilities in a definite manner and failure to provide the basic resources necessary to achieve objectives. Organisational weaknesses such as these affect a business so profoundly that it is doubtful whether an effective profit improvement programme can be carried through without a soundly based organisation structure.

Organisational change

The key factor in organisational change is specifying the purpose and objectives of the company as a whole and breaking them down into functional objectives. Given an effective division of the work, the managerial resources then need to be stretched to their reasonable limits. The managers must know the levels of performance expected from them and receive the appropriate support and information. All this is basic and self-evident, but the problem is often that organisation structures have a tendency to drift into a self-perpetuating logic which is seldom questioned except when a major crisis breaks. Whenever management consultants are called in to advise on a general management problem however, and whenever there is a company take-over, it is an odds-on chance that changes in organisation structure will follow.

A profit improvement project group is not an appropriate vehicle for examining either organisation structures or general management routines. Only a small group of main board directors can take on this responsibility. It should be made clear to the profit improvement group that these subjects fall outside the scope of its consideration except for lower level organisational changes which are below the level of the executives in the project team.

Management system and routine

Tied up with the organisation structure is the way the management team goes about its business of running the company, including its planning, budgeting and review systems. The common failings in these areas are:

1 A failure to set objectives which are quantified, time-dated and broken down into functional objectives.
2 The production of corporate and long term plans which are not integrated with the operating arms of the business.
3 A heavy reliance on internal data sources and insufficient attention paid to external markets, suppliers, and inflationary trends.
4 Poor evaluation of management effectivenss.
5 An acceptance of 'loose' budgeting techniques.

It falls outside the scope of this book to deal with planning procedures other than to point out that during times of increasing inflation when markets and suppliers are disturbed there is an even greater need for the planning process to be followed through and to be updated more quickly. No element of inflexibility is suggested here, rather that the necessary changes in course dictated by inflation need to be made within a preconceived framework. Managers must react calmly rather than violently to unexpected developments.

Evaluation of management effectiveness by activity studies

To assess the effectiveness of management and staff carrying out non-repetitive operations, the most frequently used technique is activity sampling. The aim is to identify the time spent on critical aspects of the work in order to reorganise the system or routine with the object of reducing the time spent. It has an obvious application in work study practice and is particularly useful where large groups of people can be observed in reasonable clusters. It can be used to identify queueing time, down-time and delays, and with modification, it can be used to observe traffic flow. The study is carried out by an observer who works to a pre-arranged pattern based on a randomised statistically significant sample. He or she simply records the activity taking place at each observation of each person. Over time a picture is built up of the total pattern of work for the group as a whole and for individuals. It is necessary to secure the cooperation of the personnel involved in the study beforehand and to explain its purpose. A pilot study will be necessary in most cases in order to formulate the questionnaire accurately and to provide an indication of the likely direction of the results.

It is a matter of great concern that senior management is seldom willing to apply such a study to its own work. The really critical resource of any business is its management, every other resource such as plant, machinery, product formulations, advertising or market information can be bought or copied by competitors. A company's management is its most unique resource and it is critically important for most organisations to know how it is used. It is also a highly scarce resource, there is always more work which can be done than there is management time available to do it. One way of making extra time available is to redeploy the time spent on existing work. An activity study can assist greatly. It may throw light on duplicated effort, ineffective routines, and poor communications.

The following example demonstrates both the need and the benefits.

A food company in Amsterdam, Holland, proposed to integrate its production planning with a computer-based sales forecast. To evaluate the cost benefit of the computer, an activity study was carried out amongst clerical staff in production planning and in the research and information section. This involved a series of eight checks taken each day at selected times, for a period of six weeks, a total of 240 plots. The telephone service arranged to provide a series of alarm calls at the right times to a secretary, who would then visit the staff and fill in the questionnaires, noting the type of work they were doing at the time. In this way a pattern of their individual and cumulative workloads emerged.

The marketing director asked to be put on the study himself. He estimated the likely results before starting: the actual results are shown here with his estimates in brackets.

New product development	11%	(25%)
Customer contact	8%	(15%)
Advertising and research	10%	(10%)
Trouble shooting	25%	(10%)
General policy matters	18%	(15%)
Sales organisation	20%	(20%)
Administration	8%	(5%)

His activity was also classified as follows:

Travelling (car, train etc.)	10%	(15%)
At formal meetings, (superiors, colleagues)	6%	(5%)
At formal meetings (staff and executives)	5%	(5%)
At informal meetings (superiors, colleagues)	15%	(25%)
At informal meetings (staff, executives)	36%	(20%)
On the telephone	8%	(5%)
Writing, dictating	13%	(10%)
At outside meetings	7%	(15%)

Through this activity study he discovered to his alarm that the effect of stopping with his executives, staff, and with his colleagues to have talks about various matters as they cropped up was taking over half his time. In turn, his executives were wasting a great deal of their time with their staff, and so on.

A weekly executive meeting was arranged with a time limit set for one hour so that news and information could be exchanged between all the senior members of his staff at the same time. This meeting was not designed to take decisions, merely to keep everyone in touch with developments and to avoid the constant need for asking for information on an 'ad hoc' basis. If decision taking meetings were needed, then these were arranged for a separate time. There was no way of calculating the increase in effectiveness, but the marketing team believed it to be considerable and the procedure was adopted in a number of other departments, and at Board level.

The problem for management is to find a way of increasing the amount of time when executives are really effective. Usually this corresponds to a tiny proportion of the working day, when an executive is most productive. At other times he is involved in meetings which barely concern him, dealing with low grade administrative tasks, travelling, and handling paper work much of which could be processed for him. The 'disturbance factor' in an executive's time is considerable. The problem then is not to increase the total time he spends 'at work', but to increase the effective proportion. To take one example. Industrial psychologists can show that people generally do individual tasks better, earlier in the day rather than late although this partly depends on the personality features of the individual. Thus, if the company generally holds its meetings early in the mornings, it becomes more difficult for an executive to carry out an arduous and complex personal task later in the day. If social interaction within the company has been experienced and enjoyed early in the day, it is harder to apply the self discipline needed for a long personal task. That is why so many managers do this type of work at weekends or at home when they are free from interruptions.

Tight budgeting to contain inflation

Normal procedure for the buildup of budgets is to take each cost centre and to allow for an increase or decrease in activity during the budget period and to compare this with the current year. It is usual to allow for cost inflation. These expense budgets are then matched to the forecasted sales revenue with a net profit figure result which is itself compared to the net profit objective for the year. The costs and revenue figures are then juggled, until finally the budgeted net profit fits the objective. This procedure has been called the loose budgeting technique. At best it carries on the company in the style to which the company has become accustomed. At worst it can stifle a company's initiative, create interdepartmental strife and inhibit effective decision-making.

The tight budgeting routine proposed here is the natural extension of the Systematic Approach and is one way to ensure that a continual profit improvement programme is carried on since it is bolted into the company routine, making everyone conscious of the need for cost-efficiency. There are three assumptions:

1   That marginal opportunities for cost saving exist in any cost centre or budget.
2   That marginal opportunities for increasing sales revenue, at low additional cost, exist in any market.
3   That managers are constantly striving to improve their performance, ie obtaining greater outputs from lower inputs.

During increasing inflation, the loose budgeting technique often means that costs rise higher than expected, sales are often harder to obtain than was forecast, and that planned price increases lag behind the inflation of costs. What is required is some form of contingency built into the expense budget so that managers organise their operations in such a way that they know where additional savings are to be found if they need to find them.

The tight budgeting sequence is broken into two stages. The first stage calls for potential savings to be examined and proposed. The second stage is where the budget itself is agreed. At the first stage, managers in charge of cost centres are asked, 'How would you maintain the effective output of your operation if you had to absorb, say, 10% for inflation this coming year without an increase in your budget?'

The question can be broken down to cover sub-functions, such as plant utilisation, engineering services, sales effectiveness, order processing and so on, varying the objective to make sense for each department. Such a break-down as this is necessary to push the tight budgeting procedure down the line and in order to involve the whole management staff at all levels. Once again, it should be explained that this is an artificial question, designed to force them to think of the marginal activities with which they might have to dispense in a crisis. Usually it forces them to think of new routines and combinations of systems which will allow them to support their operations as they want but with less cost. This is the precise objective of the exercise.

A manager produces a list of his marginal activities for his superior. These are graded by size of cost reduction, ease of implementation, and by least risk to the enterprise.

The list will contain three types of savings:

1   Activities which are dependent upon decisions made in another part of the organisation. For example, if the sales department agree to an increase in the delivery lead time for customers, then routes can be altered, journeys extended, and vans, drivers, petrol and maintenance saved in the transport budget.
2   Activities which the manager regards as being of high risk if dropped. The risk is to his ability to perform the task adequately with smaller resources, or the risk to activities which are central to the company's effective operation.
3   Those expenses for which he is nominally responsible but which are incurred at lower levels of management.

The technique for dealing with the first problem, of diseconomies between departments, is to put the interdependent managers together in a group and to challenge the group as a whole to produce savings. There will be immediate trade-offs between managers, and once a manager is exposed to the costs which his activities create for other managers, new routines will often be devised to minimise them. Some of these new routines may need thorough study before they can be implemented but they may result in a long term payoff. This is part of the continuous profit improvement programme.

The risk problem in reducing the effectiveness of the operation belongs to the manager's superior. Lists of these cost saving opportunities should not be regarded as proposals, they are merely the identification of areas for potential saving. The decision must be taken out of the manager's hands. Furthermore, he cannot be penalised if the operation is not successful. Under the tight budgeting procedure the budget cannot be used to 'punish' managers who fail to contain their expenses. There must be a central contingency fund so that central management can put back into the operation any expenses which are seen subsequently to be necessary to the operation. There are marginal opportunities also for increasing sales at every level of the organisation, by applying different amounts of energy and altering the direction of the effort. This is discussed more fully in the chapter on sales organisation.

The tight budgeting technique allows a company to survive the perils of inflation with a nil growth forecast. It applies equally well to a growth company since once the draft budgets are prepared after all the economic opportunities have been identified, the necessary additional funds for expansion and to exploit growth possibilities can be added. Furthermore, it will be easier to see these additional funds for what they really are, investment opportunities. It will also be easier with this method to measure the resulting costs and profits from expansion moves, than it would be under the loose budgeting technique. The latter allows a company to drift into expansion in a general way without separating the current expenses from the new investment.

Companies can modify this technique in their own ways to suit their own management styles and operations. The effect of this approach to budgeting is that a management team will:

1   Know the short term objectives to achieve.
2   Know about the interacting effect of their activity on other departments.
3   Focus upon the need to conserve cost and to product profit.
4   Understand the purpose of additional funds for growth.

Senior management will also have a knowledge of where its managers regard the 'soft' areas of the business to be, where, in their view, there may be additional savings to be made in a crisis. If inflation causes unexpected pressure on profits, the company now has a central contingency reserve which is written down to profit as the year proceeds.

It is tempting to propose that the profit improvement programme should be tied into a management by objectives system (MBO). Where MBO is already safely installed within an organisation, it is easy to build profit improvements into the objectives when setting and reviewing stages. Some companies however, cannot handle the MBO system well, particularly authoritarian organisations which tend to use it as a means of imposing their will upon their management team. This causes inflexible attitudes, aggravating reviews and an emphasis on defensive postures, the worst things that can happen during a profit improvement programme. The problem is to modify the MBO system to suit the company, recognising that the important task is to secure the active cooperation of managers in a situation which may threaten their responsibilities, and to ensure an active response to crisis and a favourable climate for change. Within the MBO system, the following features are entirely consistent with a profit improvement programme:

1   A critical review and re-statement of the company's strategic and tactical plans.
2   Definition with each manager of the key results and performance required from his unit as a whole, a decision in which he participates and concurs.
3   Management information and control data provided in a form and at a frequency which will assist in making more effective decisions.
4   A systematic approach to management training and development so that managers can build on their own strengths. The needs of the managers must be recognised.

The tendency in the MBO system review procedures is to focus upon a man's weaknesses in management and upon his performance failures. This has a very serious affect upon morale. There are very few senior managers who can handle reviews with their subordinates with the psychological and verbal skills required.

The management audit

A management audit carried out by an experienced individual or team can be very productive if it is focussed upon the right areas. The auditor must be a sound problem analyst and capable of grasping the essentials while retaining an independent viewpoint. He must be secure in the confidence of management at all levels and be able to relate his experience to their problems. He must be experienced across a wide range of functions and be objective and impartial. This generally calls for a mature but energetic mind.

The management audit is likely to be successful if it is directed at the following points:

1   The appraisal of management information to ensure that relevant and timely information is reached all executive levels and is acted upon.
2   The appraisal of systems and control procedures, budgetary techniques and standard costing.
3   Appraisal of the business organisation structure to ensure that it is sound, meets the aims of the business and effectively uses the human resources.
4   Appraisal of the technical competence of the staff, equipment and other physical facilities required.

The audit is less likely to be successful if it attempts to appraise the individual performance of functional operations, or concerns itself with assessing the economic or market environment for the company. For these tasks a specially recruited Profit Improvement Team is required.

Reducing management service costs

One of the most important tasks for senior management is to see where internal service costs can be reduced or replaced with more flexible services outside. As organisations grow in size they tend to adopt one of three philosphies. They build all the necessary support services into the organisation structure as an overhead cost. This brings them under full direction and control but increases the overheads considerably. Or they purposely keep a small management team which then decentralises as much as possible, buying support services from outside the organisation as and when required. Or they have no firm policy on services but allow individual functions the freedom to grow internally or buy outside services as they are needed.

During the initial profit improvement stage it is necessary to review this policy. A company with a high fixed cost suffers most when the market turns down. On the other hand it is often difficult to control a thoroughly decentralised organisation. For every service and support function it may be necessary to ask, 'Is there an alternative service from outside which is adequate for the purpose but less costly?'

The following services are normally built into company operations as an overhead. In some companies it is possible to reduce the level of the internal service so that its primary task is to buy the service competitively from outside.

1   Research and development.
2   Product design.
3   Graphic design.
4   Engineering.
5   Freight.
6   Storage (warehousing).
7   Market research.
8   Library services.
9   Personnel selection.
10   Advertising.
11   Public relations.
12   Sales promotion.
13   Accountancy.

The advantage of using outside services in these areas is that a company can turn them on and off as conditions require it. There may be other advantages such as being able to call upon a wider range of expertise; or the ability to call upon increased resources in a period of heavy demand. The disadvantages are, that the outside service organisations are not so familiar with the business or with its personnel, they may not be immediately on call and, used continuously they may be more expensive than the internal service. In any business however, with a highly variable seasonal pattern of activity, or whose scale is not sufficient to keep an internal service fully stretched, it will pay to examine how the manning of internal services can be reduced and supplemented from an outside source. The supreme advantage is that it makes the outside service more accountable for results when the service is in a competitive situation and when each task has to be separately costed and evaluated.

Checklist for buying outside services

Two key criteria

1 Do they completely understand the problem and all operative factors and influences?
2 Do they know how to use the appropriate techniques?

The advantages of using outside services

1 Reduces overheads ie less full time staff required.
2 Often results in more professional objective and accurate work than if conducted in house.
3 Some projects are of such magnitude or technical difficulty that they exceed in-house resources.
4 Many larger organisations provide wide ranging and international capabilities.

How to select outside companies

1 How long has the firm been in business?
2 What is the experience and background of its principals and client-service executives?
3 To what extent would the senior executives be committed to working on the project — part time — full time — or are they to provide supervision?
4 What evidence is there that the firm is financially responsible — bank references — credit references or a financial statement?
5 Who are the firm's previous clients and what do they say about the firm's work? Would these clients give repeat business to the firm?
6 How well does the firm's personnel get on with the client personnel?
7 How much experience, direct and indirect, does the firm have in the specific problem areas under discussion?
8 Does the firm's proposal reveal a clear and complete understanding of the problem? Is its proposed approach to solving the problem logical, thorough and likely to produce the results that are wanted?

9   Itemise what information, assistance, and resources the firm will require from the client in the course of the project.
10 Itemise what the firm commits itself to furnish as evidence of completion of the project.
11 Specify how any disputed points will be resolved.
12 Are the firm's time and cost estimates for completing the projects reasonable?
13 Will the firm assign the company full rights to the use, at the company's discretion, of any materials developed during work on the project, whether or not suitable for copyrights or patents?
14 How much, when, and in what manner will the firm be paid for its services upon completion of the project.?

A written agreement is required for a successful outside project. The agreement should cover:

1   A schedule including the major steps in the project.
2   The points of contact in both the client company and in the outside company.
3   The desired quality eg supervision required, validation etc.
4   The extent of sub-contracting contemplated by the outside, firm for what specific steps, and the people of firm(s) who will be used.
5   The penalties for non-performance, eg not completing the exercise by the agreed date.
6   The form that interim progress reports and final presentation would be taken.
7   The fees, and when the fees will be paid.

6

Financial Accounting and Cash Management

During inflation, even money itself is a wasting asset.

Most business crashes used to come about because firms traded at a loss for too long. Nowadays, and in years to come, many profitable firms will crash because they failed to manage their cash properly.

Continuous inflation has the following effects upon business:

1 Credit becomes more difficult to obtain, and creditors pursue outstanding debts harder.
2 Loans become expensive and difficult to obtain unless backed by realisable securities.
3 Markets are distorted, forcing companies to become more flexible in their operations.
4 Traditional accounting practice does not show a true picture of a company's situation.

The financial accounting function within an enterprise therefore has a critical role to play during inflation, one which may determine the survival of the company itself. It can directly influence trading profits only in a relatively minor fashion. In this area it does not have the same leverage on decisions which affect revenue earnings and expenditure, such as can be claimed by marketing for example, or by management accounts by its influence on pricing and operating decisions. It can however directly affect the profitability of capital expenditure decisions and plays a central role in cash management practices.

Inflation accounting

Clearly its basic function is to provide an accurate and up-to-date picture of a company's asset and liability situation. In the past ten years we have witnessed the widespread use of discounted cash flow as a technique for evaluating the true profitability of capital projects over a span of time which allows for the cost of money and which can be adjusted for inflation. Now, some form of inflationary accounting is certain to be introduced as a standard practice in most large organisations. In the long run, this is likely to be accompanied by adjustments in tax legislation by Western governments, to allow for inflationary accounting. No doubt each government will come to its own various decisions on the matter separately from decisions by other governments. This will continue to have the combined effect of disturbing the efficiency of their trading companies and leaving enough room for the specialist in multi-national organisations to move money around the Monopoly board of tax havens in the world without, it might be added, helping their own country's inflation problem very much.

Inflationary accounting is concerned broadly, although not exclusively, with the valuations of fixed assets, stocks and work in progress, and borrowings. The traditional method of depreciating a new machine assumes that a new one will cost no more than the old one – in fact machinery prices can more than double in less than five years, as new and sophisticated models are introduced to the market. Any reserve in the accounts based upon the historic method of depreciation is nowhere near large enough to pay for its replacement. (The UK industrial companies' pre-tax profits were 30% higher in 1973 than in the previous year. Of the year's increase in gross trading profits, 60% was the result of stock appreciation alone. Once this item is adjusted then company profits in general are seen to have fallen by 14% between the first and second half of the year). Unless the financial accounting system shows up the true state of affairs, a company may make dreadful decisions based on profit figures which are simply too optimistic. This is particularly true in a situation of rising inflation, when estimates of future costs are always too optimistic. The company may become committed to risky projects when its real capacity to support losses is nowhere near enough.

Shops, stores, factory sites, office buildings, other properties and land however, escalate in times of inflation, largely because there is a rising demand for a relatively stable resource. Consequently, inflationary accounting practices must update these values year by year, otherwise the profit figure in terms of the return on capital will be overstated. In this respect the valuation of stocks is especially difficult. With a fast stock turn the valuation is easy since sales are matched continuously against replacement stocks. In enterprises where there is a long manufacturing lead time, some form of indexing system is necessary. In commercial businesses, such as insurance and banking, the indexing system may have to be applied to the net monetary position since this is, in effect, the 'stock' of the company. Clearly if the value of money is eroding at 10% per annum or more, then the monetary value of company assets must reflect this. The technical problems may be immense, since a single index figure to cover all adjustments, for assets and liabilities including borrowings, is not likely to be enough. Nevertheless, the fact that a problem is difficult to deal with does not make it any less vital.

How inflation accounting works

The following example was prepared in order to illustrate how the figures of a company may be presented in the supplementary current purchasing power statement. It is not intended to be a step-by-step worked example of the calculations involved. The example is reproduced from *Accounting for the Inflation Spiral* by Arthur Platt, which appeared in the June 1974 edition of *The Director*.

The figures in the current general purchasing power basis columns were arrived at by converting the corresponding figures in the historical basis columns by reference to the changes in the Consumer Price Index between the dates of the original transactions and the end of 'this year'. The current general purchasing power basis figures for both this and last year are measured in pounds of purchasing power at the end of 'this year'. The Consumer Price Index at the end of this year was 139.3 and at the end of the previous year was 129.0.

Profit before taxation

Figure 6.1 demonstrates how the difference between profit on a historical basis and on a current general purchasing power basis is made up.

	This Year £'000	Last Year £'000
Profit before taxation (historical basis)	215	205

Adjustment to convert to current
purchasing power basis

Stock

| Additional charge based on restating the cost of stock at the beginning and end of the year in pounds of current purchasing power, thus taking the inflationary element out of the profit on the sale of stocks | 37 | 25 |

	This year £'000	Last year £'000
Depreciation		
Additional depreciation based on cost, measured in pounds of current purchasing power, of fixed assets	25	17
Monetary Items		
Net gain in purchasing power resulting from the effects of inflation on the company's net monetary liabilities	(12)	(10)
Sales, purchases, and all other costs		
These are increased by the change in the index between the average date at which they occurred and the end of the year. This adjustment increases profit as sales exceed the costs included in this heading	(10)	(7)
	40	25
Profit before taxation (current general purchasing power basis at end of year under review)	175	180
Adjustment required to update last year's profit from last year's pounds to this year's pounds	___	15
Profit before taxation (current general purchasing power basis at end of this year)	175	195

Figure 6.1   Adjusting profit before taxation from a historical to a current purchasing power basis

Stating the company's results and financial position

In Figure 6.2, the loan capital at the beginning of 'this year' amounted to £200 000. £200 000 at the beginning of this year is equivalent in purchasing power to £216 000 at the end of this year (because inflation has been 8% during the year). As the company's liability to the providers of loan capital is fixed in money terms this liability has declined during the year in real terms from £216 000 to £200 000. This reduction of £16 000 in the company's obligation in terms of current purchasing power is included in the net gain on monetary items of £12 000 shown in Figure 6.1.

	Historical basis		Current general purchasing power basis	
	£'000 Last Year (1)	£'000 This Year (2)	£'000 This Year (3)	£'000 Last Year (4)
Results for the year				
Sales	1920	2110	2190	2134
Profit before taxation	205	215	175	195
Taxation	82	86	86	89
Profit after taxation	123	129	89	106
Dividends	60	60	61	65
Retained profit for the year	63	69	28	41
Financial position at end of year				
Net current assets	490	556	561	533
Fixed assets less depreciation	558	566	700	714
	1048	1122	1261	1247
Less: Loan Capital	200	200	200	200
Deferred taxation	39	44	44	42
	239	244	244	258
Total equity interest	809	878	1017	989
Ratios				
Earnings per share (p) (based on 500,000 shares in issue)	24.6	25.8	17.8	21.2
Dividend cover (times)	2.1	2.2	1.5	1.6
Return on total equity interest (%)	15.2	14.7	8.8	10.7
Net assets per share (£)	1.6	1.8	2.0	2.0

Figure 6.2   **Summary of results and financial position adjusted for the effects of inflation**

The technique for financial accounting according to the systematic approach

'How can we improve our return on capital by 5% after allowing for inflation, and improve our cash flow?' A question of this kind, adjusted to the circumstances of the company and directed at executives in the financial accounting function, will provoke answers in the following broad areas, which accountants directly affect.

1 Delaying payments to creditors, negotiating better credit terms.
2 Pursuing debtors more vigorously.
3 Reducing bad debt risks.
4 Speeding up cash management operations, reducing borrowings.
5 Cutting departmental costs and the costs of external services.
6 Reducing the capital base of the enterprise.

The techniques for carrying out these objectives borrow from techniques for increasing the efficiency and cost-effectiveness of general management. This is particularly true of questions relating to clerical productivity and to systems improvements. Related to financial accounting, possibilities of increased efficiency through mechanised accounting have already been over-explored by IBM and others. It will be more productive to focus upon some of the lesser known human situations which occur in accounting and which can be improved.

Negotiating credit

For example, it is a frequent failure of purchasing departments to secure long credit terms from new suppliers at a time when the supplier is most anxious to do business. This is a failure of company organisation, in that this objective is generally not built into a purchasing officer's job specification. Furthermore, he is seldom measured and controlled by his performance in this area. This is a matter for financial accounting to deal with. They, and they alone, have the skills necessary to show a purchasing officer the profit effect of his credit negotiations. They have the data available to them, but generally allow the situation to develop, although in many cases they themselves should become involved in the negotiations at an early stage. After a new supplier has been lined up and the prices and delivery agreed, it is too late for the financial accountant to try to talk terms. Indeed fast payment is often promised to suppliers by a purchasing department even though the company creditors stand at nine weeks or more. Purchasing officers then wonder why they receive so many complaints about payment from suppliers, when they may have caused the problem in the first place. If the company's accounts payable usually stand at nine weeks, then it must be the job of the purchasing officer to negotiate 8–10 weeks credit and it is the task of the financial accounts department to show them the need. Suppliers are often more worried about security and regularity of payments than they are about the actual time negotiated and taken. A clear policy on this point reduces administrative costs, increases borrowing capacity from suppliers and directly improves profits. At the core of the problem is better communications and training.

Pursuing debtors

The running battle between sales departments and accounting departments over the question of customer credit delights every management consultant, because he knows he is going to find it in nearly every company he studies. The same battle is fought over the same ground using the same arguments from the same entrenched positions in nine companies out of ten, no matter what their size and the nature of their business. It is a pity because there is money being lost in the process. The arguments run roughly as follows:

The salesman says: the accountants are pursuing the customers too vigorously for money, causing complaints, losing sales, creating bad will and generally being unhelpful to the sales effort.

The accountant says: the sales department is opening too many accounts of doubtful credit rating, offering terms which are too generous, and is generally unhelpful in dealing with the credit risks they are responsible for causing in the first place.

There is truth in both arguments. The issue can only be solved by examining the question from the customer's point of view. The normal customer has a right to negotiate the best terms he can obtain, and expects the company to meet the sales representative's commitments after the normal credit checks have been taken and his business has been cleared as a credit risk. He expects the company to make good its promises of delivery, service and product. When he has a genuine complaint he expects the company to attend to it quickly, and to put right any agreed error. If the customer complains of not being treated in this way, then he will withhold payment because that is the one certain way in which he can engage the company's attention. No accountant should complain about this behaviour, since the accountant's own company is behaving in an identical manner with its own suppliers. We are dealing here with normal customers behaving normally, not with bad credit risks or customers in financial difficulty.

The answer can be divided into three stages: first, the salesman must negotiate clearly and preferably in writing, the terms of business which his company operates. This must be understood by the customer and by his bought ledger accountant. Any variation of these terms must be processed through the supplier's sales ledger and account collection routine. Second, the invoicing and statement of account procedure must be handled efficiently and quickly so as to operate within the customer's own accounts payable and invoice clearance procedure in time for the start of each month's routine. Third, at the first sign of an overdue account, particularly in the early months of dealing with a new customer, a procedure must be operated quickly and should assume in the first place that the account is being withheld for payment owing to a possible complaint or service error. The entire process of account collection must recognise that there is a human communications problem involved which does not lend itself to a heavy handed procedural routine which is recognised for what it is by the customer. The salesman is right – it is difficult to obtain sales and very easy to lose customers – equally, the customer is right to demand the service that he has been promised. At the same time he must pay his bills.

An efficient routine combined with some human understanding, plus a little ingenuity, will be sufficient to bring overdue accounts into line, as the following example demonstrates.

A South African electrical goods manufacturer follows up its debtors with a letter from the customer service officer – a lady – when the account is one week overdue. In the letter, she offers to deal with any complaint immediately it is telephoned through. Additionally, customers are reminded of the terms and asked to pay within 10 days. At day 11, if the cheque has not been received a telephone call is put through to the customer's bought ledger department; the progress of the payment is noted and agreement is sought on the date by which a cheque will be received. These two procedures are enough to cover over 97% of debtors and will pick up all the sales and service complaints. The customer service function is situated within the sales department and is paid for from the sales budget. To keep the costs down therefore the sales force is thoroughly trained to negotiate terms with the customer's accounting function at the initial order stage.

To flush out the remaining 3%, one trained girl calls the financial director of the customer, or deciphers the name of one of the men responsible for cheque signing. She tells the director's secretary that it is a personal call. When she can speak to him personally, she asks for his assistance in solving the problem. They agree upon a date for payment, she makes one final call if the cheque does not arrive by that date. After that the company sues. The company offers 30 days credit. The debtors stand at an average of 39 days. The company's goodwill is high. Their competitors' debtors stand at approximately 11 weeks. The cost of the additional pressure through the telephone, including staffing is more than offset by savings in stationery and postage using the normal system and the marginal cost of borrowing for the outstanding debt during the period.

The use of planned personal telephone calls to recover outstanding debts works well when the individual sums are fairly large and when the credit lines in an industry are long. This is also a key method of identifying bad debt risks early, since information gleaned about the customer and any evasive behaviour can often be detected by a telephone girl trained to pick up such cues and signals. Agreements over payment made personally by telephone but not kept are a sure sign that more forcible action must be taken quickly; it is a well known phenomenon that the risk of bad debts remaining unsettled goes up in geometric proportion to the length of time they are overdue.

A bad debt on the books is more than a loss of sales revenue, more than a loss of gross profit contribution if nothing is recovered. It is a straight payment out of net profit. If the normal net profit rate is 10% on turnover, then the saving of one bad debt is worth ten times its value in sales.

Speeding cash management

To improve company liquidity a number of options are available. During inflation a company must work its cash as hard as possible, both to improve liquidity and to increase profits by a reduction in borrowings. While it is true that during rising inflation it is better to be a borrower than a lender because of the decrease in the value of money, the truth is that it pays to be neither. It is better still to use the money to make more.

The principal moves are, first, to ensure that a pricing system allows for charges to be presented for work in progress or for deliveries that are not necessarily complete, in the way that a printer, for example, might charge for the production of artwork, typesetting and making blocks, even before the delivery of the final job. Many companies cannot price in this way, but there are equally others who could negotiate staged payments and choose not to do so.

Second, the invoicing and statement of account procedure must be handled swiftly at the end of each month. If there is an accounts lag in this area, it may be necessary to close the account down a little before the end of the month, allowing the invoice department a little more time to handle the work.

Third, bank all receipts immediately and never permit usable funds to lie idle even for so much as a day.

Fourth, develop and use sources of money that are not only cheap but flexible and readily available. In this way, the cash balances available are kept to the minimum required for the day to day operation.

Fifth, never pay accounts until they fall due; negotiate longer term credits with suppliers; take advantage of cash and payment discounts but only when they exceed the cost of borrowing money over the time it could take to pay the bill. Generally they are higher, and it is worthwhile to take them.

Effective cash management cannot work properly without a cash plan. A cash flow budget is the first step required to indicate the likely forward cash balances month by month. Cash flow planned years ahead is a very useful guide to likely long term capital requirements. Often capital budgets are approved and loans are obtained for money which companies find later that they cannot use. This is generally because the assumptions have been made on the very conservative basis that all capital requirements would be financed from outside sources, without allowing for cash flow contributions. Long term cash flow plans, although often wrong during rising inflation also make loans easier to negotiate since bankers can see that the company is planning to work its money hard.

Previous Year: Year:

	Oct.	Nov.	Dec.	Jan.	Feb.	Mar.	Apr.	May	June	July	Aug.	Sept.	Oct.	Nov.	Dec.
Estimated monthly sales invoiced															
Estimated receipts from sales (45 days delay from invoice) monthly income				—	—	—	—	—	—	—	—	—	—	—	—
Payments to suppliers for goods (Goods received 4 months ahead of sales, paid for 2 months later – i.e. cash moves 2 months ahead of sales).															
Monthly payroll, Social Security etc.															
Other monthly payments (fuel, transport, advertising, rentals etc.)															
Periodic payments:															
Capital purchases															
Fees and royalties															
Taxes															
Sundries															
Total outflow of cash each month.	—		—	—	—	—	—	—	—	—	—	—	—	—	—
Income versus outflow, monthly.			—	—	—	—	—	—	—	—	—	—	—	—	—
Cash in hand at 31 December previous year			—												
Cumulative – i.e. monthly cash balance	—			—	—	—	—	—	—	—	—	—	—	—	—

Figure 6.3   Forecasting cash flow

Reducing the capital base of the enterprise

One of the quickest methods of increasing the return on capital is to reduce the amount of capital involved in the business, or at least to limit its growth.

During inflation, a company's greatest need is for its assets to be flexible. Specially designed and produced machinery which cannot be resold puts a company in a very high risk situation if there is a turn down in the market. It forces the need for turnover, this need increases the amount of discount offered in an attempt to win trade while competitors make similar moves. Increased discounts offered to a market declining in consumption must be paid for out of net profit. At the same time as company profits decrease, borrowings increase and the cost of borrowing depresses profits further. It would be far better to have disposable assets which can be traded if necessary, such as land, non tailor-made buildings, standard machinery; even cash is better than a long term fixed asset in time of trouble. It may be wasting away, but at least it can easily be pushed into something more profitable.

Leasing instead of buying machines, doing without support services such as building units, transport, data processing, making heavy use of outside suppliers instead of internal services, all these provide a greater flexibility and enable a company to concentrate its affairs upon the activities which it does well and which make the company profit. It is important, critically important, for a company to recognise which of its activities and which of its assets are highly productive and which are not. Those activities and those assets which are not fully productive should be eliminated, even if the company is a little smaller and leaner as a result. The resultant surplus energy concentrated on highly productive areas of the business will produce profits in excess of any earnings which might have been made from the marginal activities.

7

Unfreezing the Cost Accounting Process

The first operating function to realise the damaging effect of rapid inflation will be management accounts. The often uneasy framework on which cost standards are based look more doubtful than ever. The disparities become more variable. The business looks as if it is going out of control and may be doing just that.

During inflation, standard costs go awry very quickly as a result of market distortion damaging sales revenue, added to changes in the normal product sales mix, supply shortage causing rapid introduction of new suppliers of materials at variable and higher prices, and when the general inflation of costs is spread unevenly, in effect and in time, over the expenses of the business. This compounds the normal problems of management accounting in which costs are often based upon shaky assumptions masquerading as matters of absolute truth.

The systematic approach to the cost accounting process

Where a company's management accounting function is ineffective, this department, rather than any other must be put right first. No profit improvement programme can operate without costing data which is provided quickly and accurately. Management accounts is the one department which may have to be enlarged significantly when a continuous profit improvement programme is built into a company's operations, while over-harsh economies in this area can be dangerous.

No company starts an ineffective cost accounting system on purpose, it grows that way. A bad system arises for the following reasons:

1   It does not react to cost inflation quickly enough.
2   A simple costing practice which suited the business when it was small and simple, is no longer sufficient when it is large and complex.
3   A system based upon the extrapolation of historical costs becomes badly distorted during inflation.
4   Management accountants accept standard rules of thumb without questioning the principles on which they are based and the aims in view.
5   Other functional managers have too little understanding of the methods by which costs are calculated and cannot deal with cost allocation arguments.
6   Some large costs, such as materials, are very badly controlled.
7   There is a poor reconciliation process with financial accounts.

The primary purpose of the Systematic Approach technique, within the management accounting function, is to examine each of these potential problem areas and to unfreeze men's minds from the existing procedures.

Systematic Approach methods

The problem lies in the formulation of the original question into a specific objective for a group of management accountants to consider. A more effective management accounting system will not affect profits directly, by itself. The effect will lie in enabling managers to make better decisions more quickly and to understand more of the cost implications of their decisions. It is best to focus the attention of the management accounting team on the problem of providing ideas for the improvement of the costing service in three areas:

1   The accurate identification of changing costs in products, product groups, markets, key customers, operations and processes.
2   The control of these costs when they are rising, particularly within material usage and in distribution.
3   The provision of information for effective management decisions.

Ideas put forward in answer to the first question, that of identifying costs accurately, will pay particular attention to picking up cost changes more rapidly and in the provision of faster feedback from the organisation. If the result of this work is concentrated in detail upon the 20% of purchases which account for 80% of value, then the volume of additional costing work will be limited to that where it is most effective.

    Ideas put forward to induce greater control of costs will relate to the setting up of systems to record and track the actual flow of expenses within cost centres and the usage of materials, and to providing more detailed breakdowns of variance costs such as variations in, materials usage, the yield of output, direct wages, labour efficiency, volume, machine utilisation, expenditure, discount and prices, and so on. Many of these key variances will need breaking down into fine detail particularly those which are large and volatile.

Finally, the question of making the cost accounting system more effective in guiding management decisions clearly relates to the range, level and frequency of information required by managers, the degree to which managers use and are controlled by the data and their general knowledge and comprehension of the techniques of the management accounting function. This also brings into question the way in which the costing operation is handled within the company.

Costing operations

It is tempting to suggest here that many companies have elaborate and speedy costing functions and are satisfied with their performance in this area. But by itself a wealth of detail provided frequently may be harmful, in that it creates information 'noise' so that managers find it difficult to extract the relevant data. Equally, however perfect the system looks, there are managers down the line who do not understand it and would make better decisions if they could. The head of the costing function often knows that many of the assumptions involved in the standard costing procedures are arguable. Two questions alone will demonstrate the point. Ask a head of management accounting for the basis of his judgement on machinery depreciation; if it is based upon the formula agreed with the taxation authorities, (in which case it is not enough to provide a reserve for replacement), or if it is costed on a straightline basis with a given sum allocated year by year (in which case the costs allowed for repairs and renewals in the later years must be increased), or if it is based upon some other arbitrary method. Alternatively, examine how a company's property and land values are continuously updated in the costs. There is no doubt that the answer will be that some rule of thumb procedure is used. During rapid inflation the basis of these procedures needs to be examined, even in the most elaborate and trustworthy costing function.

The more common costing problems are as follows:

Historical costing: during times of inflation, the forward ratios based upon historic costs will be wildly adrift from the realised costs, emphasising the variations. The reasons for variations are not as easily identified in a historic costing system as in standard costing based upon estimates.

Marginal and direct costing: at least this avoids the problem of allocating the bulk of overheads. When marketing, distribution and selling costs can take up over 50% of the selling price however, as they can in many product fields, then clearly the products incurring a heavier weight of marketing effort are being treated more favourably than those which are easier to sell. In multi-product companies it is very dangerous to base management decisions upon gross margin calculations alone, net profit returns vary wildly between products and the product range must be costed down to net profit from time to time, to examine the sales and distribution cost allocations.

Standard costing: avoiding some of the problems both of historical costing and of marginal costing by estimating future costs. Three basic difficulties here involve the setting up of an integrated measurement process to compare costs with estimates, the impact of sales variations on margins, and differences in material purchase prices, particularly during shortages.

The costing of materials. In manufacturing companies, materials will absorb the highest proportion of costs, but this sector is probably the most neglected in terms of cost control. In many companies, particularly those using a very wide range of differing types of material from various sources, even the basic necessity of an adequate system for analysing purchase invoices, material requisitions and stock records leaves much to be desired. True, the problem of keeping track of a wide range of materials when prices are swinging wildly is very difficult. In times of escalating inflation, nothing stays stable for long and standard costs need reviewing frequently. Additionally, as manufacturing processes becomes steadily larger and more complex, it is extremely difficult to record and keep track of all the hundreds of bought-in components and indirect materials and to see where they go and how they are used. The tendency to lump ever-increasing proportions of cost on to an indirect overhead charge is one of the main flaws in providing accurate product cost information.

In some industries there is a very poor attempt to reconcile the actual material usage compared to the estimated usage rate. Poor housekeeping in the production plant which means waste materials lying around the on the floor and pilferage, wreak havoc with material costs and destroy expected yields. Reject goods, scrap, and damaged goods should all be separately costed. Good cost control in this area highlights waste and keeps excessive costs down.

The further problem with costing materials is the valuation method used for stock, particularly when long manufacturing lead times are involved. Costing stock on the basis of the first item into stock being assumed to be used up first (FIFO) is logical and corresponds with the movement of stock. But it does overstate profits during inflation. Using the last-item-in-first-item-out system (LIFO) has the advantage of charging production with costs near the current rate, but this penalises profits very heavily. A standard price system works well whenever the price and supply situation is fairly stable and the cost standard can be expected to be maintained for some time. Probably the best system overall is to use a weighted average cost but it substantially increases the number of calculations which must be made. Practice inevitably will vary from company to company. There is sufficient evidence nonetheless, to show that even when materials are costed down to two decimal places, the figures contain many assumptions which operating managers in functions other than management accounting should be aware of.

Labour costs. At least the waste of materials is fairly visible, usually a heap of scrap in the corner of a yard. The waste of labour is a whispery intangible thing which is seldom there to be seen.

On the other hand some sources of waste labour are easy to perceive; strikes, excessive overtime, or groups of people standing idle. The costing difficulty is to identify those moments of idleness when men are waiting for machines to complete their run, when they are collecting tools or waiting for materials, or taking instructions. In most jobs, these factors will add at least 10% to the labour cost, even on high speed production lines. In some jobs where there is batch production or skilled labour involved, or the working conditions are uncongenial, such as in a noisy factory or outdoors in bad weather, the excess labour cost may be 100% of the standard. Work study often fails to allow sufficient for idle or waiting time and tends to set 'ideal' times while the expected standards may be much lower. Add to this the problem of labour incentives and the deliberate manipulation of the process in order to secure more benefits for labour such as additional overtime, then the labour costing problem is very difficult. There is the further problem that with many skilled and semi skilled jobs it is not the total hours spent 'at work' which matter, it is the relative productivity of a small proportion of the time which counts. If, on occasional costings, the total labour cost is thrown against this highly productive proportion, then some very interesting results emerge leading to management decisions which concentrate upon increasing the efficiency of this proportion.

Overheads and central costs. As marketing costs escalate, and as manufacturing plants become more highly automated, the larger proportion of cost is shifting from direct to indirect charges.

The problem of overhead cost allocation is really one of measuring whether and how much of each cost should be allocated to current production, and whether the company could achieve better value for money with the remainder. Costs such as corporate planning, research and development and personnel management are difficult to allocate to profit centres and it is a matter of judgement as to how the company's profit would be affected without them. The other difficulty lies in allocating central costs in decentralised companies. In strongly profit motivated divisions, particularly where there are financial incentives for good performance it may pay a senior manager to argue more about the way his central overhead contribution has been computed than about his real business of making money. If the contribution has been determined by the size of divisional turnover, then this will work against divisions with high material costs and in favour of service operations and those with a ratio of high profits to low turnover. There will be a distorted effect in the charges to divisions and the decision may have little bearing upon how much demand is made upon the central company service. Its only logic is that there is a flat standard system which brooks no argument.

The following example shows how a company with high fixed overheads is much more sensitive to changes in sales volume than any other.

Two companies operate in the same field. One, A, relies heavily upon outside services and suppliers of components. The other, B, has a widespread management team and is more heavily geared to its own production.

Rapid inflation distorts the end markets, and there is a down turn of 10% in consumption. Which company is most affected? Both are making 10% net profit.

| | A | | B | |
	Before	*After*	*Before*	*After*
Sales	100	90	100	90
Direct costs	70	63	30	27
Fixed costs/overheads	20	20	60	60
Net profit	10	7	10	3
Change on net profit:		−30%		−70%

Note: It is equally true that if the sales increase, then the company with high fixed costs benefits more in additional profit. Furthermore, some fixed costs and expenses such as salaries and advertising are easier to cut back than others such as plant or property.

Figure 7.1   The danger of a high fixed cost business when the market turns down

It is better to allocate central company contributions on the basis of the gross margins earned rather than on turnover, but this is not necessarily sound either. It will assist the division with low salaries and fixed costs; other divisions operating in more competitive markets and requiring a wide range of skills applied by many people will have a further burden to pay in terms of additional central company contributions. (See Figure 7.2.)

One solution might be (as in Figure 7.2, 4) to set up each division and the central company itself with a set of profit objectives. The central company itself

1	*Division 1*	*Division 2*	Central
			manage-
Sales	1 000 000	1 000 000	ment
Direct costs	650 000	150 000	overhead
Overheads	300 000	700 000	costs
Net profit before central			100 000
management charge.	50 000	150 000	

The results of the Two Trading Divisions before the Recovery of Central Management Costs.

2	Division 1	Division 2
Sales	1 000 000	1 000 000
Direct costs	650 000	150 000
Overheads	300 000	700 000
50% of central management charge	50 000	50 000
Net profit	NIL	100 000

Central Management Costs allocated on the Basis of Turnover

3		Division 1		Division 2
Sales		1 000 000		1 000 000
Direct costs		650 000		250 000
Overheads		300 000		700 000
Central management charge	30%	30 000	70%	70 000
Net profit		20 000		80 000

Central Management Costs allocated on the Basis of Share of Overheads

4		Division 1		Division 2	Central manage-ment
Sales		1 000 000		1 000 000	required
Direct costs		650 000		150 000	cost
Overheads		300 000		700 000	recovery
Central management charge	20%	22 000	80%	88 000	including
Net profit		28 000		62 000	profit objective 110,000
Net profit		28 000		62 000	10,000

Charges and Profits if Profit Objective is ten percent and Central Management spend eighty percent of time on Division 2.

Figure 7.2   How central cost allocations affect net profits

'trades' in the sense that its services of financing, policy co-ordinating, long range planning and project management as well as any specific management services it offers such as training, personnel management, estates management, and so on are 'bought' by the trading divisions. Although the central company is dealing with a closed market of its own divisions and subsidiaries, it prices its overall service on two levels. The first is based on the 'value' of its service, estimating what proportion of its work is taken up by the various operating divisions, and the second is based on 'what the market should bear', meaning that the more powerful profit-making divisions should provide extra cover for the new fledgling units which are assisted in their early years with a low central management charge. The system also encourages central management to expand the group operations so as to spread the central charge around more operating divisions. In effect, it means that the central company has some duty to justify itself and its charges to operating subsidiaries, but in practice it can also manipulate divisional capacities to earn profits, particularly by favourable allocation of charges to new operations, while the more powerful divisions bear the additional burden. It may also be important for the central company to hold a contigency reserve, additional to profit which can be written back to any division which needs additional funds for growth, or to meet some unexpected development. In this way divisions are paying something for their security should the trading conditions become difficult.

Transfer pricing. Another major problem which is a management accounting concern is the price that one division charges another for the work it does. In decentralised companies which have interdependent businesses this can be a most difficult problem, one which leads to a great deal of internal strife and, unless handled carefully, a loss of profit-earning capacity. It is a well known feature of many large multi-product organisations that the most difficult buyers they have to sell to are those that work for their own group.

The basic principles of sound transfer pricing are fairly clear:

1   The prices and costs should be allocated in such a way as to reflect an accurate measure of efficiency. One company's profits should not be so vastly inflated by favourable pricing from another division that the other divisional profits are severly depressed.
2   Transfer prices should not allocate to a division a greater profit than it would be capable of earning on its own without the synergistic effect of working with another part of the group.
3   Sound transfer prices should ensure that any action which is taken to increase the total group profit does not decrease the division's profit.

Where goods are passed from one division to another in the form of raw materials or finished products there are three pricing systems in common use. These are:

Paying the market rate for the product. This means that the buying division is paying full cost for the product more or less at the rate it could obtain outside the firm. The difficulties are obvious. The division may pressurise the group to allow it to buy outside thereby depriving another division of the income, the buying division may feel resentful that the full profit has been obtained by another division and may increase demands for a higher level of service. The supplying division, finding itself with a most profitable customer within its own group, will lack that much incentive to develop business outside, which is harder to obtain and less profitable to serve.

Paying the marginal cost of the goods only. This has the reverse effect, in that only the direct cost of the product and limited overheads are taken by the supplying company which then has a tendency to drop the level of service and become generally resentful and difficult to deal with. In an extreme case, if the supplying division has no other outlet for its production, then it can be made to look so unprofitable that the group can consider closing it down. This would be a poor group decision, since apart from the loss of group contribution, the buying company would now have to pay full market rates for its product, making its loss of contribution very considerable.

The most equitable system should involve a sharing of the combined profits between the two divisions as a result of the synergy. For example, the supplying company could take no net profit from the deal, and could pass on all the genuine savings in marketing, sales and distribution. Beyond that it could share some of its research and development charge and other central service charge with the buying company. This leaves the buying company with a product which is cheaper than it could otherwise purchase, and it leaves the supplying company with some overhead contribution from the business. The system can be operated with a general group discount applied to the normal sales price which might be 15% or more.

Where purchasing officers are contributing heavily to the profitability of their division and resent having their hands tied by having to buy certain products from within the group, the group policy might allow them to purchase a proportion of their requirements from outside suppliers, perhaps up to 20%. This gives them some leverage on their own company suppliers who are forced to compete for the business to some extent, and it gives them some experience of the market place. The competitive advantages of the practice may outweigh the loss of contribution from the business which goes to outside suppliers. Indeed, purchasing officers are often only too happy to come back to the group supplier when they find they receive a poorer level of service from outside.

If a purchasing department can make out a case to show that their overall group profit contribution can be increased if they are allowed to buy a particular requirement outside – perhaps because of very favourable terms offered which more than outweigh the profit contribution to the supplying company – then the policy should allow them to be able to make out the case, for group management to finally decide.

8

Improving the Purchasing Operation

Over two-thirds of the total expenses of the average manufacturing company are made through purchasing department orders, yet the purchasing officers choose probably less than 10% of the suppliers.

The first step in controlling inflation is to control purchasing, and to institute an effective system of supplier search and evaluation. To increase the control of costs of key materials requires close work with selected suppliers which is where the technique of supplier development comes into play. Since inflation is often accompanied by product and material shortages, a range of purchasing techniques needs to be developed for dealing with reluctant suppliers.

The mindless neglect of the purchasing department function in most manufacturing concerns is the source of more inefficiency than any other factor in business. The purchasing officer tends to be relegated to the status of middle management, pressure to select particular suppliers is put on him by senior technical staff, his personal authority to purchase is limited to low value items and the Board of Management makes major decisions. As a result, it is no wonder that purchasing officers become cautious, and passive. Nonetheless, it is these rather than anyone else, who will be the professionals operating in the purchasing area. Promote a chief purchasing officer to the Board of Management with full powers to review all supplier evaluation and screening procedures, and the additional profit resulting from this one move may be enough to cover one year's inflation.

The buying company faces a number of dedicated, well-motivated, highly trained, self-seeking experts probing its purchasing weaknesses all the time. These salesmen seek to get behind the purchasing officer, and to manipulate the

Assumptions: both companies are making a 10% net profit, and the materials saving does not cause an increase in indirect costs — such as heavier purchasing department wages.

	Company with High material cost		Company with Low material cost	
	Before	*After*	*Before*	*After*
Materials	80	76	20	19
Direct labour	5	5	5	5
Indirect costs	5	5	65	65
Net profit	10	14	10	11
	100	100	100	100
% Increase in Net Profit		+40%		+10%

Figure 8.1   The effect of a 5% saving in materials costs

organisation structure to get what they want. There are twenty books written on selling, for every one written on purchasing. The successful salesman can go right to the top of his company, the successful buyer can reach middle management, at best, in most concerns.

The Systematic Approach to purchasing operations

'How can we reduce the cost of purchases by 10% while at the same time improving supplier efficiency?'

The use of the Systematic Approach within the purchasing area will reveal literally hundreds of good ideas, once the basic procedures have been analysed.

Previous profit improvement studies within purchasing have put up the following projects:

1   Concentration on searching for alternative suppliers for essential goods and continuous technical evaluation of offers.
2   Concentration on technical effort on the 20% of suppliers which account for 80% of the expenses.
3   A regular stock check to identify redundant and waste stock.
4   Initiating quality control checks for rejects and shortages at goods inward stage and applying quality control checks in the supplier's company.
5   A survey of existing suppliers to establish from them how prices could be lowered by changes in company routine. This may reveal a number of flaws

in the buying procedure including buying the wrong product, ordering in uneconomic batches, too many rush orders, and so on. If the purchasing company can help a supplier save money then they should be able to negotiate a reduction in cost without damaging the supplier's net profit.

6 Offering prompt payment in return for cash discounts or negotiating new terms of payment.

7 Altering product design to fit standard components. (One company asked its component supplier to carry out a value analysis check on the company's products thereby reducing the purchasing bills by 30% through eliminating non-standard items and also finding a further 10% savings in manufacturing cost. The supplier gained new business on other lines and increased his own profitability.)

8 Improving the stock control and re-ordering system. The most frequent cause of rush orders at high prices is a bad stock control system or a production planning system which links the sales forecast to manufacturing but fails to notify sudden shifts in demand to materials procurement.

9 Improvement in company communications and involvement of the purchasing function in product elimination decisions. Poor liaison with purchasing departments when eliminating products can mean the carrying of very heavy over-stocking of wasted materials, particularly materials with long lead times and high stock levels such as packaging.

10 Placing guaranteed orders for volume, calling off and paying when delivered, thereby enabling supplier to manufacture in economic bulk and hold in store.

Purchasing effectiveness

In recent years there has been a good deal of research work carried on in Western countries relating to industrial buyer behaviour. Most of this work has been done to serve industrial marketing techniques, and little reaction has been experienced so far within purchasing functions. From this work several useful concepts have emerged, each of which requires close study by a purchasing company for maximum effectiveness:

1 The emergence of the Industrial Buyer Behaviour Model.
2 The concept of the Decision Making Unit.
3 The concept of the Task Approach to Buying.
4 The Techniques of Supplier Evaluation.
5 The idea of Supplier Development.
6 Buying Strategies in conditions of short supply.

The use of the Systematic Approach can be applied to each of these areas in turn.

Buyer behaviour model. Several ideas exist about buying behaviour models for consumer and family purchases. But the industrial buyer differs from the consumer as a buyer in that he operates within an organisational framework and is a member of the Decision Making Unit. Unlike the consumer, he is paid to make purchases for others. Clearly, industrial buying motives are dominated by rational considerations such as cost, quality and service factors, including continuity of supply. At the same time, purchasing agents and technical specialists within the organisation have personal goals and ambitions and the choice of a particular supplier may assist them in the achievement of these. Indeed, if the chief executive of the company suggests that the purchasing officer might try a particular supplier which is run by a personal friend, it is very difficult for the purchasing officer to resist the temptation to buy if the new supplier's offer is near comparable to the existing supplier. Then once installed as a supplier to the company, it is very difficult for the purchasing officer to drop the supplier because he knows that the chief executive will wish to know why. His freedom to act in the best interests of the company is curtailed by his desire for personal recognition and commendation. Purchasing departments are constantly pressured by people elsewhere in their own organisation who use a variety of techniques ranging from gentle persuasion to outright coercion. Equally there are numerous cases of suppliers being introduced to companies by technical specialists, more for reasons of personal satisfaction than for reasons of economy and efficiency. This happens at some time in every single company without exception, however good the buying procedures.

The model of industrial buying behaviour therefore suggests that the corporate buyer attempts to steer a middle course between satisfying his own needs and those of the organisation. The degree of his susceptibility to emotional and persuasive arguments will vary according to the nature of the product, its importance to the organisation and the relative strength of the two drives within the buyer.

The Decision Making Unit. A study published in the UK called 'How Industry Buys'[1] demonstrates clearly that people are concerned with industrial buying decisions who lie outside the purchasing function as well as those within it. For example, the purchasing officer is strongest when repurchasing materials and negotiating with existing suppliers; he is weakest when plant and equipment purchases are being made. These latter purchases are influenced more by operating managements, production engineers and boards of management. Decisions to purchase component parts on the other hand, are more influenced by design and development engineers and operating managements, with the procedures varying from industry to industry.

The decision to search for a new supplier is more often initiated within the organisation, although the purchasing department is generally asked to submit lists of potential suppliers and to handle first stage screening. The purchasing department is therefore of greater importance at the early stages of initiating inquiries, whereas evaluation is carried out more often within technical and operating functions. The final choice of new suppliers is usually made in the upper reaches of the company organisation, often at board of management level. Once the final choice has been made it is generally processed through the purchasing department which places the order.

During this process, the purchasing officer will generally represent his department to the supplier's salesman as being of primary importance in the decision, whereas its true role may be little above clerical status. Equally, this is why industrial sales and marketing techniques are developed in such a way as to train salesmen to go behind the purchasing officer and contact the technical management of the company, where decisions really count. Technical and operating management, not trained in buying, is generally more gullible than experienced purchasing officers. They often over-specify and they frequently prove bad judges of economics because their own budgets are often not influenced by the purchasing decisions they take since the costs are borne in another function. They frequently resent changing suppliers and are seldom directly involved when the suppliers service is inadequate. This creates purchasing inertia, and a passive purchasing department. A sound purchasing policy is one which encourages the search for new suppliers. It should also be resourceful in locating new small suppliers which can be developed to suit the needs of the company.

The task approach to buying. Industrial buying studies[2] show that buying decisions can be classified into three basic types: New Task, Modified Rebuy, and Straight Rebuy. With New Task, a great deal of information is required since there is little previous experience. Generally a high degree of preference is given to potential suppliers either known to company personnel or to professional colleagues employed in other firms. Pressure of time between the decision to go ahead with a new design and the required production date causes a need to restrict the search to better-known companies. This limitation can be a great failing when by extending the investigations a better purchase can be made in terms of technical quality, price, service or credit terms. Clearly, a wide searching procedure at this stage and an orderly evaluation of offers will contribute handsomely to profits in time.

Modified Rebuy may be caused by some change in an existing supply situation, or change in internal events. The effect of successful profit improvement projects will be to cause new suppliers to be evaluated as value analysis programmes are worked through. Purchasing departments are important at this stage since they already have the technical competence to negotiate. Studies show that if alternative suppliers offer products of similar technical acceptability, the decision is then influenced by the purchasing department. The purchasing department's strategy is to obtain two, preferably three, supplier offers of equal technical competence so that buying leverage can be exerted on the suppliers during negotiations. With straightforward Rebuys, the purchasing departments are generally left to conduct negotiations. Often an 'approved list' of alternative suppliers is available and the purchasing task is to negotiate the best terms between them. Most company purchases fall into this category and the degree of attention paid to an individual purchase is determined by three factors:

1   The degree to which the product is essential to the purchasing company.
2   The level of risk perceived in the purchase situation.
3   The proportionate value of the product to the company expenses as a whole.

Supplier evaluation. During the 1960's the US Department of Defence initiated many new procedural practices in value analysis and in supplier evaluation procedures for companies supplying the American forces. One device, called the Contractor Performance Evaluation Programme records centrally the past performances of the major defence contractors in meeting their commitments. Another, called the Life Cycle Costing in Equipment Purchasing System is an attempt to compare offerings, by comparing the total cost of buying, using, and maintaining equipment over its life. The true cost of any purchased item includes its impact upon building or storage costs, depreciation and life, renewal and repair, the requirement for indirect materials and labour such as special oils or special maintenance, and so on.

	Supplier A			*Supplier B*			*Supplier C*		
	'73	'74	'75	'73	'74	'75	'73	'74	'75
Quality Ratio (40 points maximum)									
Price Ratio (35 points maximum)									
Service Rating (25 points maximum)									
Composite Rating (1100 points maximum)									

Source: Gordon Brand, *The Industrial Buying Decision*, Associated Business Programmes, London, 1972.

Figure 8.2   Supplier evaluation rating.

Rating Systems for suppliers (See Figure 8.2) are generally intended to calculate the costs over the full life of the equipment supplied. These fall into three classes:

1 Prevention costs.
2 Accident costs.
3 Failure costs.

Prevention costs refer to costs incurred in preventing failure to meet specification; Accident costs refer to the expense involved in checking that the requirements such as inspections and laboratory tests have been met; Failure costs refer to the costs of rejects and rework, machine down-time, loss of production, excess labour cost and so on which result from actual failure.

The system usually involves a formal weighted points system applied to suppliers. A rating on quality will show the proportion of quality control rejects. The rating on price shows the relationship between net delivered prices after discounts, payment terms, and delivery costs, together with an evaluation of price increase. The rating for service is a subjective assessment of the proportion of promises kept by suppliers.

Supplier development. The idea behind supplier development is that the buyer's role is not only to select but often to create a satisfactory source of supply. The most up-to-date purchasing departments now include cost accountants and value analysis engineers whose task is to work with buyers and with suppliers to rationalise designs and to develop suppliers manufacturing resources to suit the company.

There is a need for supplier development when:

1 Products or parts must be specially manufactured and are non-standard.
2 Unusual requirements in specification or service or the use of unfamiliar material has no ready supply source.
3 Available sources of supply are too distant.
4 Production capacity is already fully occupied and the company is unwilling to extend it though willing to contract-out the work.
5 The potential supplier is unwilling or uninterested in the business, and a new source must be created.
6 The continuity of supply from regular suppliers is in doubt.

According to studies which have been carried out, notably in Canada,[3] the development of small suppliers when the buying organisation is relatively strong has been very successful for both parties. Although the larger supplier's financial resource, research and technical strength make him an attractive target for supplier development by a smaller concern, considerable patience and persistence may be required to overcome the large company's reluctance to commit itself to a relatively small project. The studies also revealed that purchasing officers often lack appreciation of their role in supplier development and that the initiative may have to be developed within the technical and operating departments of the business.

The key to successful supplier development is to have patience in negotiation and to understand the project from the other man's point of view. The needs of the supplier must be identified and satisfied as much as the needs of the buying company. In this case the buyer turns salesman, a job for which he is often well suited. (In a behavioural sense the buyer is carrying out exactly the same task as the salesman. They are both pressured, both need to reach an acceptable solution, each weighs up the offerings of the other and uses 'game-play' techniques to 'win' his objective, both need to listen to each other and to initiate new discussion. The two jobs are exactly the same.)

Successful supplier development needs therefore:

1   Good faith on both sides.
2   A commitment to meet the other party's needs.
3   The provision of technical assistance.
4   Financial or other management assistance to the supplier.
5   A clear undertaking as to continuity and exclusivity of business in the event of success.
6   A clear undertaking of the financial responsibility to be borne by each party in the event of failure.

Buying strategies during shortage of supply. Materials shortage will continue in many fields. In some, where the increasing use of the material is outstripping the rate of replacement, the supply will run in cycles of slump and boom. In others, such as some minerals, the supply situation will steadily deteriorate as we gradually diminish the world's finite resources. The supply of goods derived from these commodities will also be affected in the way the plastics industry was affected during the Arab oil crisis. Again, inflation will cause some firms to switch their production to more profitable work, narrowing the sources of supply of the original products. Others may go out of business altogether. In some countries, inflation plus economic recession, may add up to a disruption of the social order, to civil disturbance and strikes. This will disturb markets and supplies. Clearly the sources of supply of a company's essential materials and components need to be secured. Many purchasing officers will be faced with reluctant suppliers. Consequently, the techniques for persuading salesmen to sell may sound novel now but may become essential in the future.

Some work has been done in this area of buying from reluctant sellers.[4] There are two types of situation to be dealt with:

1   A limited supply situation.
2   A preferred-customer strategy adopted by suppliers.

Temporary or chronic shortages of goods are a commonplace in every country of the world, and are more prevalent in under-developed countries. Suppliers may force customers to queue for the product, or price up their products to the limit the market will bear, or ration the product. They will certainly reduce their customer service and sales levels, and customers may find themselves having to undertake many of the services previously provided by the supplier. They may be forced to collect, pay cash in advance, conform to certain suppliers policies in the use of the goods, and so on. The only limit on the way suppliers will use such forcing techniques is the extent to which supply may become plentiful in the future and they may have to compete for business once more.

Clearly, under these circumstances, the buying company must analyse sellers motives, work out propositions which are likely to appeal to the supplying company, and generally behave like a salesman trying to win an order. The key to the technique, as with selling, is to understand and be informed about sellers motives and needs, and then to work out propositions which offer them more advantage than they can obtain elsewhere. In the future, relationships with suppliers of key materials which may become short must be carefully nursed by the buying company, rather than by the selling organisation.

The supplier who is reluctant to sell because he wishes to maintain a preferred customer situation uses either one of two techniques:

1　He establishes certain qualifications for buyers, such as minimum order lots, prepayment, or applies conditions as to the use or re-sale of the product.
2　He undermines the customer by being difficult with service, applying long delivery times, or supplying in some inconvenient form, or by simply ignoring purchasing orders.

The buyer who wishes to buy from a reluctant seller has a choice of four main techniques he can apply:

Coercion: he can coerce the supplier and attempt through force or through the exercise of authority to obtain his demands. Lawsuits, injuctions, threats to influence other customers or to create adverse publicity for the supplier, to withdraw other business, to take the issue to the chief executive of the supplying company — all these are coercive techniques. They need to be carefully handled in view of their effect upon any future relationship between the two organisations.

Inducement: he can attempt to induce the supplier to comply by offering something of value to the other company. Paying a premium price, offering a reciprocal deal, offering sole supplier rights. In these and in other ways the supplier is offered an incentive to supply.

Education: he can attempt to educate the supplier, through changing the sellers beliefs or values. He may be able to show the supplier how the growth prospects for his company or his industry will affect the future demand for the goods. He may offer a supplier some kind of development relationship designed to show him how he can improve his own business, and so on.

Persuasion: he can attempt to persuade the seller to do business through showing how his natural interests are served by the transaction. He may be able to demonstrate that his company is a reliable customer, that it settles its accounts quickly, that it is reasonable in its behaviour towards suppliers, that the future interests of the end users or of society at large are served by the supplier complying with the company's request, and so on.

In general, buyers must learn how to handle the growing sophistication of sellers and to identify the range of appropriate buying techniques which they can apply. The days when buyers were tough individuals who wanted twice the quality at half the price delivered tomorrow on long credit are going. Industrial relationships between sellers and buyers are becoming more integrated and the view that the only healthy contract is one where the interests of both parties are satisfied is growing in importance. Equally, once the purchasing function is regarded as a profit centre of the company in its own right and the chief purchasing executive is promoted to the mainstream of senior management, then the purchasing function will become more active in developing alternatives and more effective in the contribution it makes to company profits. It may mean the difference between failure or survival.

References

1 *How Industry Buys*, Hutchinson, London, 1967.
2 P. J. Robinson, C. W. Farris, *Industrial Buying and Creative Marketing*, Allen & Bacon, Boston, 1967.
3 *Improving Purchasing Effectiveness through Supplier Development*, M. R. Leenders, Harvard University, Boston, 1965.
4 P. Kotler & S. Levy, 'Buying is Marketing, Too', *Journal of the American Marketing Association,* January 1973.

9

Increasing the Value of the Output

Every company carries useless costs. Every company can improve the quality of its performance. The effect of rising inflation is to increase redundant costs and reduce the quality of performance. Where this affects technical production, the loss of profits can be very considerable. Inflation disturbs profitability and damages cash liquidity. It creates a disruptive effect among both suppliers and within markets. Fiscal measures and other government inspired actions create further disturbances which may have their effect upon organised labour. The result may be industrial action, demands for higher wages, increased absenteeism, strike action, or to make the recruitment of staff more difficult. All of these possibilities have the following effects upon production:

1 A profit or cash crisis makes its impact upon new projects and risk ventures, it depresses investment in new ideas for growth. New product development gives way to rationalisation.
2 Variable and unexpected changes in costs of materials and labour, plus the use of alternative suppliers and materials creates havoc with product costing and with product specifications.
3 Market disturbance, even allowing for the sudden emergence of growth opportunities which inflation sometimes reveals, creates rapid changes in the sales mix and this in turn affects the mix of items to be manufactured.
4 Sudden material shortage disrupts production.

Added to this, there is the continuing problem that unnecessary costs are carried in all manufacturing and service enterprises. Whether these are a large or small factor depends upon the degree of simplicity of the production operation; the degree to which attention is paid to value analysis as an on-going exercise, and to the productivity of labour, materials and capital.

To deal with these problems requires concentrated attention on the basic elements in productivity, continuous appraisal of systems and procedures, a continuous review of specifications, and the flexibility to adapt to changing circumstances quickly. It means turning the company inward to focus upon its efficiency, rather than outward upon growth. The normal causes of unnecessary costs carried by organisations are due to management inefficiency such as complacency, a lack of planning, a lack of pressure or a lack of training. There is also an inability to apply considerations of value, perhaps due to inadequate information, poor communications or shortage of ideas. Equally there are human considerations such as strongly held beliefs, ingrained attitudes and habits, or simply a desire to play safe. In all of this the real weaknesses are human ones: systems are ways in which people are organised to work together and must be tailored to support human endeavours and not to inhibit them. Various types of analytical and measurement techniques which can be used to increase productivity have been very well documented in technical journals and books and no purpose would be served here in describing them again. Indeed, most of the techniques have rather specialised application within specific industries and work operations. But the general principles of value analysis and productivity improvement which can be applied to all businesses, large and small, manufacturing or service, must be dealt with here. The intention is to provide a focus upon the main areas in which profit improvement programmes can result in benefits.

Value analysis

In a manufacturing business the one technique which will emerge above all others when a profit improvement programme is introduced will be value analysis, if it does not already form part of the company's on-going operation. Most products are over-engineered in one way or another, particularly high volume and profitable products. The problems occur within the development stage itself. When a new product is introduced to the market several flaws are inherent in the process. All technical departments build in error tolerances to their estimates and plans, just in case their judgement is wrong. The process engineer allows for a slightly lower rate of machine output than he believes he can obtain. The cost accountant builds small 'tuck-ups' into his estimate of costs. The marketing department plans for a conservative level of sales which they hope to exceed. The purchasing officer relies upon estimates from reliable suppliers, rather than upon the cheapest he believes he can obtain. The development technologist allows for a slightly higher packaging specification to overcome problems of breaking, spoiling, damage, or contamination during transit. In companies where such decisions are irreversible, where machinery and plant must be designed just for the product in question so that these factors cannot be altered, then a value engineering programme is required at the development stage. This involves examining all these factors before the product is put on to the market in order to hammer down the anticipated costs. The design of any product always results in compromises of function, reliability and manufacturing method, and there are always pressures of time and ineffective liaison between departments. It is these areas that the value engineer attacks.

Value analysis applies itself to the problem of the existing production output in three ways:

1   To reduce prime costs, while maintaining value.
2   To promote greater cost consciousness amongst staff and management.
3   To promote inter-departmental cost savings and co-operation.

Value analysis therefore is a remedial technique applied to existing operations while value engineering is essentially preventative.

There are four types of 'value' which have been well documented by many authors:

The Use Value: this concerns the basic function of the product and identifies the properties within it which help to accomplish the function.

The Cost Value: this is the total cost of the materials, labour, overheads and other expenses involved in making the product.

These are the two primary value areas for attack, but there are two others of importance to a greater or lesser degree, depending upon the type of product. These are:

The Esteem Value: These are the properties which the product has which make it attractive or desirable to own. This is very high in cosmetics or in the production of hi-fi· equipment, and very low in the production of petrol or electricity.

The Exchange Value: this is the property or quality of an article which enables it to be exchanged for something else. Cars are a good example, where Volkswagen and Volvo have for many years traded upon their reputation for high second-hand value.

The value analysis procedure follows the path of most problem solving techniques. It starts by gathering the essential information, subjecting the product to a searching scrutiny of all its aspects, leading to the second stage which speculates about possible alternatives. The critical task is to identify the basic functions without which the reason for the product would not exist. This involves asking a series of questions about each part of the product — anything up to twelve in number:

1   What is it?
2   What does it do?

3   What does it cost?
4   How many parts?
5   What is the value of the function?
6   What is its primary function?
7   What else would do it?
8   What would that cost?
9   Which of the alternative ways of doing the job shows the greatest benefit in 'cost value', or 'use value'?
10   What effect would these alternatives have upon 'esteem value' or 'exchange value'?
11   Which ideas are to be developed?
12   What other functions or specifications must be incorporated?

Once the chosen idea has been evaluated it then needs to be implemented by the organisation. The Systematic Approach acts extremely well in setting up aims for a value analysis group and in generating alternative ideas. The use of other creative problem solving techniques is widespread at the idea generation stage.

Introduction of value analysis

To introduce a company to value analysis for the first time involves instructing staff and management in various departments about the basic techniques and philosophy including practical working sessions on the company's existing product line. Practical experience is an essential part of value analysis training. It may be useful to have a value analysis engineer situated within the purchasing department so that the search for alternative suppliers can be focused upon changes in product specifications. The benefit of organised value analysis is that it demonstrates better than any other method an alternative specification which can be adopted in case of supply shortage or disruption of product costs. The easiest way of avoiding a supplier's price increase is to change the product formulation so that a cheaper material or component may be used, without affecting the basic quality of the product. These alternative and acceptable formulations however, must be known to the company beforehand. By providing the company with a number of stand-by alternative procedures and by focusing upon cost questions, value analysis provides a company with its essential flexibility during rising inflation.

One of the greatest weaknesses is that 'quality' as perceived by the engineer or technical specialist is totally different from 'quality' as perceived by the customer. The customer may appreciate the company offering in terms of the delivery service or the aesthetic design of the product, compared to competition. At the same time the engineer's perception of quality is related to the performance of the materials or the complexity of the manufacturing process. To an engineer it matters that he has managed to invert the law of nature to produce the thing in the first place. To the customer, it might seem a high risk purchase if the product is difficult to make.

Since inflation will have the effect of pushing some businesses close to the financial wall — some through it in fact — then the subject of value analysis must be related to business survival generally. Value analysis engineers are very determined that their work should maintain the existing level of performance for the product and not damage it in any way. One of the effects of a profits squeeze however, particularly when prices are constrained by legislation, is to cause companies to deliberately degrade their products in order to maintain profits. This cannot be helped. A continuous value analysis study will be most useful for this kind of decision since it will immediately show the alternatives which are available for the company to exploit with only marginal effects upon product quality. In most companies, the packaging costs can be attacked first, followed by wider quality control specifications and the use of lower grade materials. This is dealt with in more detail in the chapter on product planning, and current pricing legislation must be taken into account for rules which may forbid the practice.

Control of a value analysis programme

The control of a value analysis programme is important. The general pattern varies with the size and complexity of the company and the management resources it can put behind the effort, but the basic stages are:

1   The value analysis plan, shown as a sequence of projects to be studied over a given time period.
2   The publication of this plan with a detailed time-table for those staff directly and indirectly affected.
3   The measurement of the progress and the noting of any departures from the plan during the course of the work by the project leader.
4   The evaluation of results. This is a very important stage when a comparison of actual results with original estimates is required to judge the accuracy of observation and performance.

The use of critical path analysis in a value analysis plan is very widespread and is absolutely essential for complex and time consuming projects involving long lead times and many external variables.

Increasing the productivity of labour

Generally speaking value analysis is directed at increasing the value of materials and of component parts through product redesign. Productivity studies are related more to studying the human aspects of production and the processes involved.

		Taking the savings	Increasing the output by 11%
Material cost	40	40	44.4
Direct labour cost	20	18	20
Indirect cost	30	30	30
Net profit	10	12	16.6
Output	100	100	111
Increase in net profit:		+20%	+66%

Assumptions: The company's net profit is 10% and the direct labour cost is 20%. Automatic handling can save 10% of the labour cost; should this saving be taken or should the output be increased? (A 10% reduction in labour cost converts to an 11% increase in output.)

Figure 9.1   A profitability comparison between reducing labour costs and using the spare capacity to increase output.

To reduce labour costs involves the study of five main areas of work:

1   Identifying the productivity area of any element in production.
2   Reducing the frequency of performance at any stage of the job.
3   Changing the methods or equipment which personnel use in the work.
4   Eliminating idle time, over-lapping work, over time and duplicated work.
5   Establishing standards of performance for departments, managers and staff.

In mechanical terms the question usually resolves itself into some form of condensing operation or the use of standardised parts or systems. For example, analysis of all the cartons and containers will generally reveal many shapes, sizes and specifications. Where these can be standardised it will make for easier handling, easier loading, often easier stacking, purchasing in bulk, lower stock levels through faster turnround of empty carton stocks and so on.

Again, a study of the optimum space requirement for a production task requires an analysis of the rate and variability of output, the manufacturing route and alternative possibilities. These are weighed against the capacity and load balances of the key processes and the expectations of demand. It also involves questions of shift working, and changes in layout design.

The growing concentration of separate production facilities into high-volume low-cost operations is occurring in all kinds of industries. As technology becomes more sophisticated the gap between the efficiency of the largest producer and of the smallest producer in an industry widens. By itself, greater size does not mean greater efficiency. It increases the organisations capacity to improve profits, but beyond a certain size and complexity this benefit is lost through the dispersal of management attention and drive through various layers of the organisation and the difficulty of securing the co-operation of departments as they become more specialised. The largest organisations find a profit improvement programme difficult to motivate and administer unless it is broken down into workable units of the operation.

Method study is so widely applied in industry that there is no point in repeating the need for it here except to point out that one of the factors which aggravates organised labour is that method study always seems to be applied to the lower level production staff and never to management. Yet its application within general management functions is likely to show a more substantial profits pay-off in terms of improved organisation for decision-taking than its equivalent application on the shop floor.

Human resource management

The human aspects of productivity are critical to profit improvement yet little understood. When labour was cheap and plentiful, when its bargaining power was limited, when its standard of living was set quite close to its aspirations, then there was little need for managers to concern themselves with human motivation.

The result of this neglect lies everywhere:

1 The use of heavy leverage techniques in wage bargaining.
2 The difficulty of recruiting certain kinds of labour.
3 The disruptions caused by industrial action, go-slows, work to rule, strikes.
4 Growing non-cooperation in achieving organisational goals.
5 Heavy absenteeism, particularly when wages are high.
6 Demands for worker participation in management.

Job enrichment. Out of a morass of industrial psychology investigations into human motivation in work situations, one theme has emerged consistently – the idea of job enrichment.

To identify what made people satisfied or dissatisfied at work, studies were carried out in a wide variety of working situations. The original study, now repeated many times and always with consistent results, asked people to describe in detail what was happening in their jobs at times when they felt unusually satisfied, interested or enthusiastic about their work. Equally, they were asked the same question related to the times when they were dissatisfied, frustrated or unhappy in their work. The answers to the questions are not mutually exclusive. In other words, the kind of thing which causes satisfaction at work is not necessarily the opposite of the kind of thing which causes frustration, and vice versa.

The work situations which people find most satisfying are generally those which provide the opportunity for achievement by the individual and recognition of that achievement. What motivates people is interesting and challenging work, genuine responsibility and scope for advancement and growth. These factors lead to enthusiasm and satisfaction. On the other hand, the work situations which are most dissatisfying to people are generally those in which factors such as company administration, human relationships, technical supervision, working conditions and pay are felt to be inadequate. These factors lack the power to motivate people in a positive sense in the way that challenging aspects of the work do, but they have the capacity for causing disaffection and frustration. People respond in one way to their tasks and in another to their environment, and either aspect is ignored by management at its peril. The neglect of this human relations aspect of work has allowed systems engineers to take out of the work at all levels much of the interest and challenge that it previously held. If people are to be motivated, then the tasks they are asked to perform must be examined and their responsibilities increased. This may involve the redesign of operations so that an operator completes the whole module of work rather than one constituent operation. Substantial breakthroughs in productivity and in labour relations have been recorded by companies which have redesigned their work in this way. By itself this is more important than supervision, communications and training.

Equally, the other aspect of a 'Job Enrichment' programme needs to be fulfilled. The pay must be satisfactory, the working conditions reasonable, the attitude of management and other factors concerning human relations must be adequate. By themselves these factors will not improve productivity, but without them productivity will not improve much.

Productivity bargaining. A job enrichment programme may lead to more successful productivity bargains although in traditional industries, where habits die hard, the road will be strewn with the difficulties of union negotiation. Companies do manage to make industrial relations breakthroughs however, despite the need for patience and perseverance. These will be all the greater in those companies where there already is a deeply entrenched management/union hostility so that the necessary trust does not exist on either side. Under these circumstances, the inflationary pressure which puts a bite on company survival may be seen to be of considerable value if the pressure of the crisis is the one thing which is required to bring management and unions together.

The favourite targets for productivity bargaining are recognised to be:

1   Amendments to existing incentive schemes.
2   Wage structure reform and job evaluation.
3   Labour flexibility.
4   Contracts with fixed terms instead of open-ended.

5   Changes in working methods such as mechanisation or shift work.
6   Over-specialisation and excessive skill rigidity.

The problem during inflation is to prepare people for change to be acceptable and at the same time to provide as much assurance as possible about job security. In a deeply entrenched situation, it may be necessary to make changes in several minor parts of the operation first so that an element of trust develops out of experience. It may be necessary to guarantee that pay adjustments will be indexed to inflation, if legislation allows this, so that the real level of earnings does not fall. Certainly this is a risk, but the pay-off is to be found in long term goodwill and co-operation, and in productivity increases. Finally, the involvement of labour and management in creating ideas for productivity improvement together, with both participating in generating ideas, is vital. The involvement of the shop floor in promoting change ideas is vital from the start. To tell them, after changes have been decided, is not only to sow the seeds of resentment but also to lose a very profitable source of profit improvement ideas.

It is people who produce profits, not systems. If management concentrates upon the people, the systems will look after themselves.

10

Improving the Product Mix to Counter Inflation

During inflation, the losers in the game of product planning make roughly the same decisions as the winners. They just get their timing wrong. They fail to cut back quickly enough or they fail to reinvest when the market is at its lowest. When inflation moderates and the world learns how to cope with it, this difference of timing will be seen to have totally altered the shape of many of the world's major manufacturing industries.

A company can make no more profit than its product sales mix allows. It can, however, fail to optimise its profit capacity. Inflation disrupts both sales and profits within the product mix:

1   By taking discretionary income from the market it directly affects sales of capital goods. In industrial markets it slows investment which affects new projects.
2   It causes down-trading in both industrial and consumer markets. People and companies switch their buying to lower price goods.
3   The effect of government action on prices and wages, or by directly and indirectly acting upon demand disturbs markets suddenly.
4   Markets are distorted by shortages of materials and goods, creating handicaps for some and opportunities for others.
5   The effect of inflation on company costs is uneven, causing greater profits pressure on some products than on others, so that the profits mix is affected.
6   Lack of cash for new investment puts pressure on new product development costs and limits the exploitation of growth opportunities.

Nonetheless, at the same time the sales turnover may be increasing with inflation and the tendency is to believe that the company is doing quite well. During inflation, it is the output figures which tell companies the state of the game, not the sales revenue figures which are clouded by price increases.

Product planning

Formal product planning is poorly understood in many companies. Yet it is vital during inflation to have a soundly constructed policy based upon a realistic estimate of, future of demand, prices and costs, and materials supply in the key markets which the company serves. Without such a plan production lines will be suddenly closed, some factories shut, labour laid off or put on short time, profits will decline, liquidity will be affected, investment will be cut back, management morale will drop — all the worst evils of a company in financial and market trouble — can be experienced simply because the problem of product planning was not thought through thoroughly enough.

This is not a dramatic over-statement of the situation. Some companies, not all, are affected directly and precisely by inflation just in this way. If inflation rises high enough quickly enough, then all companies will be affected like this, the question therefore is just a matter of the degree to which the companies product mix is vulnerable to the impact of inflation on its markets and on its supplies.

Handling the product plan is similar to having a portfolio of shares, each product being similar to an investment in some company equity. During the course of time, some shares will rise in growth or in earnings, some will decline as also will products in the range. An investment analyst will make an annual review of the portfolio and will recommend the selling of some shares and increased investment in others, plus the purchase of a few new ones to replace those eliminated. This gives the portfolio a spread for security's sake and a balance between growth and earning power determined by the investors need for one or the other. It is identical to the product range problem. This method cannot maximise the profits from the share portfolio. To do that would need detailed knowledge of the future share prices of each investment separately in order to make changes at the right time. Such prescience is given neither to man nor to his investment analyst, so the 'optimising' technique is used as described. In the light of history, some shares may be bought or sold which should not have been, but that cannot be helped.

During inflation, the stock market becomes depressed and prices fall. This happens even though some companies paradoxically enough may be announcing record profit levels, perhaps due to the inflation of stocks, as happened with the oil companies in the six months following the Arab oil embargo. The stock market recognises that this record profit is not a true sign of company health but a symptom of the disease. Within a company, climbing sales revenue from a declining output Is a symptom of the same disease. The decisions that investors make during a falling stock market mark out the professionals from the amateurs. The best ones take the following actions:

1 They cut their high risk, high capital intensive investments in those areas which are most likely to be damaged by inflationary difficulties.
2 They narrow their range of investments to those which will give them the best 'cover' even though these investments are also likely to fall with the rest. They must put their money somewhere after all, to take it all in cash means its inevitable erosion.
3 They improve their flexibility to meet sudden changes, holding more investments in short term funds and a higher proportion in cash.
4 They move their investments, where they can, into those overseas markets which are less prone to inflation.
5 They invest where they can in appreciating assets such as land or property when the prices look low enough.
6 Many of them speculate a little, searching out the opportunities which inflation creates within a market.
7 All of them are ready to move back into the market with long term investment immediately prices are very low but the economic outlooks shows inflation as being controlled. After severe stock market depression, prices move up rapidly when conditions begin to improve.

All this action has a very real and distinct parallel to product planning in every sense. The principles of action in product planning are as follows:

1 To thoroughly measure the likely impact of inflation upon all key markets and products, and to pay close day to day attention to sudden developments.
2 If the operation has to be cut back, cut it back hard though not necessarily fast, but do it earlier rather than later.
3 Offer a tighter, streamlined product range with contingency funds held to exploit sudden opportunities.
4 Develop overseas and other markets which are less prone to inflationary impact. To move from a high fixed cost manufacturing base towards a low fixed cost service organisation is one such alternative. Service organisations with low capital intensity seem to ride inflation rather better than manufacturing organisations.
5 'For new product development, speculate a little, particularly into those areas which do not tie up capital or technical resources and where there is a possibility of a small but fast payback. There are many such opportunities in the market which large companies often ignore because of their small potential in size. These become much more attractive in times of zero

growth. An acquisition policy towards innovative but small companies may be one answer.

6   Invest at the point when the market is at its most depressed, when some are saying it will become even worse but the company judges it as improving. A high market share, established at the point when the market is depressed, will pay for itself handsomely when substantial volume reappears.

It is fully recognised that these are difficult and complex operations which will often involve reorganisation that takes a long time to mature compared to the relative ease and short time scale involved in changing stock market investment decisions. However, inflation is probably here to stay for a few years yet, and the fact that it is a difficult problem to resolve does not alter either the need for this to be done or the principle basics of action. Furthermore, general increases in productive efficiency must be found of the order of between 5% and 15%, as that part of inflation which cannot be covered by price increases. To obtain this kind of return needs only marginal pressures on each of these areas.

The Systematic Approach in product planning

Using the Systematic Approach in each of these directions reveals three underlying strategies:

1   The elimination of low profit products and the orderly profit-stripping of marginal activities.
2   The allocation of resources behind the high producing products in the range.
3   The development of products which will earn profits in the near future and the development of long term projects up to the point of technical feasibility, for the time when the market turns up.

Elimination and profit stripping. Weak products, even though they may be contributing to company profit, consume a disproportionate amount of management time and energy. Owing to the management accounting practice of allocating fixed costs according to straight-line principles based upon machine output or some other standard measure, these products are always producing less profit than the accounting figures show, while the high volume products are always more profitable than they look from the figures.

This is because of the 80/20 problem. When 80% of effective results are earned from only 20% of management activity, it is clear that most of management time is relatively unproductive because it is wasted on the 'problems' of the business. In the nature of things, these problems are often the low earning, small volume, troublesome products and markets. No one will ever be able to prove how the elimination of a marginal product or activity which is contributing fully to overheads, and a little to net profit, can actually increase the gross contribution of the remaining activities. Management accountants have a habit of asking how the contribution is to be replaced when such activity is due to be dropped, and managers are often helpless in the face of such logic. The answer is, that in the short term there will be a sudden and distinct loss when the product or activity is dropped. The overall effect of dropped activities may be quite ugly in the short term. In the long term, however, the profit position will be improved because management and capital can now be concentrated upon developing and sustaining the rest of the more profitable activities which have a greater combined payoff than the elimination of marginal exercises. Furthermore if the operation is handled on a large enough scale, there will be savings to be taken in indirect costs; administration, accounting, storage and distribution,

The fact remains that there is a heavy reluctance to drop company activities unless a crisis threatens. The Systematic Approach can be used very successfully however, since it can combine the varied attention of a number of departments such as production, marketing and finance, each of whom has a vested interest in the decision. The setting up of the original question is the critical stage, which will vary from company to company. The original question needs to be determined by the corporate objectives in the area of growth, profitability, the need for a suitable long term market position and to cover the impact of inflation. These are some of the questions which might be asked in order to initiate the study.

'If we must produce 10% fewer products from our resources, which products should be eliminated and how?'

'If we must cut back 10% of our activities in production, distribution, markets, and still maintain long term profit growth, which activities must be eliminated?'

'If the size of our product range and our market position must be maintained but with 10% fewer product items, what must be done and with which products?'

The following example demonstrates how a Product Elimination Audit revealed savings opportunities for a company with a range of six products. (See Figure 10.1, page 102).

1   The effect of dropping product F was to lose some sales volume and value. But some sales loss was taken up by product E and a little by product D.

2   The gross margins in products B and A were improved. The effect of the increase in contribution flowed through directly to net profit.

3   In addition, further marginal but untraceable savings in overheads were a likely result from having fewer products.

    a   Administration and accounting.

    b   Stocks, stock control, order processing.

    c   Lower discounts and financing stock.

    d   Savings in advertising and promotion.

Product:	A		B		C		D		E		F	Total
		%		%		%		%		%		
Sales in £'000	60		50		40		20		16		12	198 sales
Material cost	24	(40)	25	(50)	20	(50)	6	(30)	9.6	(60)	7.2	
Labour cost	6	(10)	5	(10)	4	(10)	2	(10)	1.6	(10)	1.2	
Direct cost	30	(50)	30	(60)	24	(60)	8	(40)	11.2	(70)	8.4	111.6 Direct cost
Contribution	30	(50)	20	(40)	16	(40)	12	(60)	4.8	(30)	3.6	86.4 Cont.

Net profit 19.8

Product F was dropped from the range. Its sales were closely associated with Product E and, to some extent with Product D. An attack on packaging costs of Product B and the introduction of automatic handling on Product A reduced certain costs. The following cost structures resulted.

Product:	A		B		C		D		E		Total
		%		%		%		%		%	
Sales in £'000	60		50		40		22		22		194 sales
Material cost	24	(40)	22.5	(50)	20	(50)	6.6	(30)	13.2	(60)	
Labour cost	4.8	(8)	5	(10)	4	(10)	2.2	(10)	2.2	(10)	
Direct cost	28.8	(48)	27.5	(55)	24	(60)	8.8	(40)	15.4	(70)	104.5 Direct cost
Contribution	31.2	(52)	22.5	(45)	16	(40)	13.2	(60)	6.6	(30)	89.5 Cont.

Net profit 22.9
Increase in net profit: 15%

Figure 10.1 Product elimination and profit improvement

The practical criteria for evaluating products have reference to:

1   Market share.
2   The relevance of the product to the rest of the range.
3   The sales volume of the product.
4   The degree to which capital or other scarce resources are committed to the product such as management or machine time.
5   The importance of the product to customers.
6   Its vulnerability, in terms of markets, supplies or costs, to the impact of inflation or government action.
7   Sales forecasting/production planning, difficulties, short runs, etc.
8   Its influence on credit, customer discounts or bad debts.
9   Its impact upon company reputation.
10   The growth prospects in the market.
11   Its coverage of overhead.
12   The degree to which it ties up sales or service time.
13   Its impact upon costs such as waste, breakage, sales commissions.
14   Its market acceptance.

Profit stripping marginal products. The answers to such questions as these will produce a number of candidate products for elimination. At this stage there is no abandonment decision, these are still candidate products which should then be subjected to scrutiny on the following grounds:

1   How much could be gained by product modification or value analysis?
2   How far can the price be increased dramatically or the product quality be degraded, or both, either as a prelude to abandonment or in place of it?
3   How much could be gained by modifying the marketing and sales strategy?
4   How good are the alternative opportunities in this product area?
5   How much useful management time and resource can be gained by dropping the product?
6   How much in total revenue — not percentage — is the product contributing beyond its direct costs, minus any indirect costs which are incurred in marketing, selling and distributing this product specifically?
7   How much is the sale of this product contributing to the sale of other products in the range?
8   Has the market got potential for the future, and if so, what?

If the decision is to abandon the product or the activity, since we might equally be discussing the elimination of a delivery depot, or a complete production line under this review process, then the activity can be carried on under a planned profit stripping process. Every opportunity can now be taken to strip the product of its assets. This means deliberate product degradation starting with the aspects of the product which affect its functional performance least. For example, strong marketing support in the form of sales, advertising or promotion can be withdrawn without harming product value at all. The product can be taken off the price list, made in large economic batches, stored centrally and only delivered with long lead times, instead of being backed by the full battery of company service. The packaging costs can be reviewed, thinner board used, of lower quality and less of it, printed in fewer colours or the quality control tolerances in production processes might be widened to allow more rejects through. The labour costs might be lowered through manufacturing the product only to suit the production plan instead of to customer order, thereby minimising its impact on rush working costs and overtime. The materials might be cheapened or the product formulation changed. Associated with these changes might be a price change; either up, if the quality has not been seriously damaged, or slightly down in order to secure a little customer goodwill.

It should be pointed out that countries with a Price Code are likely to expressly forbid reductions in product quality. The authorities however are looking at functional performance rather than at peripheral matters associated with product costs, such as packaging. Furthermore, if a company can show that without a mild change in product quality a product would have to stand a considerable price increase, then the case is likely to be accepted. The standard rule of value analysis, to alter product formulations in such a way as to maintain product performance and not lower it, usually requires some evidence of testing before it will be accepted. This will often involve testing by independent agencies such as outside laboratories or by market research companies. If a product must be seriously degraded in quality because of a rapidly rising cost or material shortage, the case is more likely to be accepted if it can be carried out at the same time as a small price reduction. A combination of product degradation, and a price increase from a company trading with relatively high profits is likely to be refused by the pricing authorities.

Clearly not all of these opportunities can be taken. They should all be examined nonetheless since small changes here and there, made to products which have no future in the company anyway, can result in considerable profit improvement in the short term and lessen the impact when the product is finally dropped. Indeed, the savings may be considerable enough and the resulting fall off in sales small enough to hardly effect revenue, and the product can remain in the range as a healthy profit contributor.

The product elimination process. If the elimination programme is worked to a long time-table, taking each of these changes in turn then the product may stay for two or three years or more. (See Figure 10.2). During this time, plans can be laid for the orderly disposal of assets connected with the product, ie the sale of the machinery, if not of the factory itself. The product formulation itself and the brand name could be sold to another smaller organisation with a lower base of fixed costs who could sell the product as a very profitable addition to their range, an effect of only marginal consequence to the large company. In this way, there is a planned run-down of finished and part-finished stocks and of materials. To abandon products and markets as the result of a crisis decision usually involves the write-off of vast quantities of material stocks and other production assets with very heavy write-offs on the company's balance sheet. With a planned and orderly elimination this is reduced to the minimum.

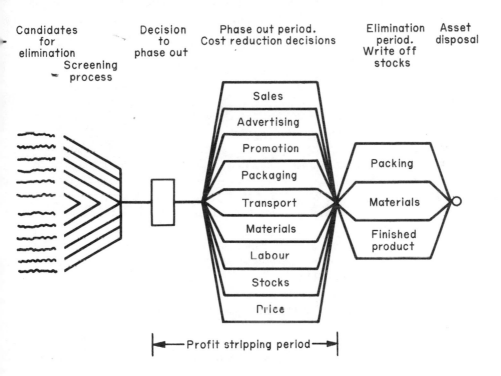

Figure 10.2   Product elimination process

Handling present High Contributors. In a multi-product company, the question of allocating resources between individual product groups is very complicated. Most marketing and planning executives make poor decisions in these areas.

The problems are compounded by several factors:

1   There are differing rates of contribution which vary from product group to product group.
2   There are different levels of sales and marketing support required for each product; this affects the costs *after* the contribution has been calculated.
3   There are different sales volume levels between product groups.

4   There are differences between the levels of scarce resource in production, providing some products with substantial capacity before the cost barriers are reached and others with little spare capacity.
5   There are differing degrees of response in the market place to levels of extra marketing effort for each product group.

Even the simplest operation, that of allocating promotional funds to only three different products in the range is extraordinarily difficult and involves a great deal of subjective judgement. With a complex multi-product operation the problem is multiplied many times.

There are five factors which should be determined beforehand, even if on a subjective judgement basis:

1   The existing production capacity and the point at which resources become limited or expensive, product by product.
2   The likely rate of market response to extra sales and marketing effort, plus the future market growth potential, including all the parameters of competitive response.
3   The abandonment of sales figures as a guide and the use of contribution figures, after direct costs, as a preliminary basis for the decision.
4   The abandonment of percentage indices (eg gross profit/net profit rates) and their conversion into true monetary values. In resource allocation decisions, working with percentages can be a very real danger and adds considerably to the confusion.
5   The attempt should be made to cost product groups down to net profit contribution, including a detailed examination of the marketing support costs in each product group.

When these factors are agreed, then sensible resource allocation decisions can be made. The use of percentages and of total sales figures are the two confusing factors. Total sales revenue is immaterial to the efficient handling of management decisions. Indirect costs are the only ones which contribute to net profit. The direct costs of materials in particular, and to a lesser extent of labour, (since most labour costs in the broadest sense, are semi-fixed, and only vecome truly variable in their allocation between individual products made on the same production line), these are immaterial to the making of net profit, since they rise up and down in line with output. Even if savings are made in material costs then these savings will flow through first to gross profit contributions and may or may not emerge into net profit after that. For example, a saving of material costs may result in increased overheads, quality control, purchasing, customer complaints and so on.

Net profit is the outcome of the productivity of fixed costs; one product with a low gross margin yield may be a high contributor to net profit because it incurs lower overheads. In this case, this may be the product to force, because the productivity of fixed costs is very high. The figure indicates how this might come about. Yet most marketing executives will allocate extra funds to those products which have a higher gross margin proportion, rather than to those which incur less management effort.

Again the use of percentage figures to compare one product with another is very harmful. A percentage is only an index figure showing the relationship of two figures. The gross margin percentage, for example, shows the relationship between total sales revenue and direct costs. In comparison with another product group, both of these variables will be different — sales turnover and costs — so the two percentages cannot be compared in any meaningful way. Net profit is simply the sum of all the costs of making and selling the product deducted from the total sales revenue. Total cash in, minus total cash out: what matters therefore are the total cash sums involved.

Finally, some judgement must be made of the relative sensitivity of each product or group to extra marketing effort. Products holding low market shares in growth markets will have a high response to additional marketing effort compared to static markets. Some of the company's oldest established products and most efficient operations will be less sensitive to development and profit improvement programmes than smaller marginal activities.

New product development. Most companies direct their research and development teams internally upon value analysis programmes and limit their investment in original research during consistent inflation. While this may be necessary for survival, some new product development work is necessary for the following reasons:

1   Most radical new products take a long time, many years in some cases, to get to marketing stage. For a company to be in a position to exploit the market when inflation rates ease, product development work must be carried through much earlier.
2   Some new products may afford short term profit opportunities with relatively low technical or capital resource.
3   A defensive marketing posture requires some new products to be introduced to maintain the company product range.
4   During inflation competitive market situations change and provide opportunities for companies to exploit.

What is really required therefore is a restructuring of product development projects to suit these aims. In companies with a high research and development cost, a method whereby more flexibility and lower cost can be introduced to product development work is also needed. In terms of re-structuring, effort is needed to direct attention away from market segmentation; producing fewer product modifications, and to direct more attention to areas where real product breakthroughs can occur. The continuing fragmentation of product effort into different pack sizes, weights, colours or slight changes of function, creates the very problem of product clutter which a product elimination programme is trying to avoid. The causes of new product failure are frequently to be found in the areas where the new items add very little customer benefit to what is already available on the market. In companies where there is production capacity to fill, or where a healthy market position needs to be secured, then this work will be necessary, but otherwise it should be examined critically.

On the other hand, work which can be pushed into developing lower unit cost products, providing a lower price to the market, can be very beneficial. Inflation does increase the attention paid to prices in a market and the company with a lower price of offering will at least receive a hearing from buyers. If this is backed by reasonable product performance then the selling argument is sound. The problem is, that the research and development effort must be directed at maintaining the levels of overhead contribution to the company's existing products, otherwise product-switching by buyers will rob one product to pay for another. Equally, serious product advantages should be pursued in development since these will always continue to be profitable and to form the foundation for long term company survival and growth. All markets are changing all the time. The product-life-cycle theory means that existing markets will ultimately deteriorate and be replaced. A company needs new product development to be certain that the life of existing markets can be extended and that replacement products are available when they are wanted.

This leaves therefore the question of the cost of research and development itself and how it can be contained, if not reduced. During the 1960's most companies expanded their markets rapidly through extensive new product development teams. Ultimately this resulted in diminishing returns, for the following reasons: the early products to be introduced to the market are always those nominated by management as being of greatest profit potential, fastest payoff and least risk. Once these profitable seams have been mined out, the returns from new product development diminish rapidly. Then growing power in product development teams creates a tendency for technical and production management to withdraw from new product involvement where once they had a major contribution to make. In technically intensive companies, the product research and development unit becomes all-powerful, limiting the power of marketing and sales functions to determine issues easily and quickly. There is a tendency for development departments to make available for marketing only those alternative ideas which suit them. Large research and development units can often create communications clutter, making management decision-taking complex and tortuous when once it was clean and open. Finally, as the cost of research and development increases, after its initial and undoubted successes, and the failure rate of new products increases, the width of the product range grows and the level of management and marketing investment behind each product in the range is reduced, often in direct proportion to the number of products.

This is not to argue against investment in new product development. If a company has had a static product line for some time, then it will pay to increase the research and development investment, and not to reduce it. It does suggest however, that the level of investment might be curtailed; that for many companies the reversion to a straight marketing/production decision on new products with limited technical development support might be preferable to any existing slow and cumbersome approach.

Indeed, many companies operate quite successfully by copying competitors' new developments as quickly as they appear. They monitor competitors performance, identify the weaknesses and quickly develop a strategy to launch with their own product version, with much of the groundwork done for them. It is recognised that a company will not be likely to develop fundamental new ideas this way but they can sometimes overcome this limitation by a careful acquisition policy of buying out small companies with successful ideas which lack the resources to exploit them. At least the ideas will have had the problems ironed out of them and the marketing uncertainties will be reduced to known factors.

During inflation, the normal risk of new product marketing is too high to be acceptable, except under conditions of very low investment. There is seldom a shortage of really good ideas in existence in most markets. There are many which are not being exploited properly. If the wheel had been invented during a time of rapid inflation, the chances are that it would have failed to sell because people would have been too concerned in protecting their interests in log-rolling. The time to introduce the wheel would have been when inflation eased and buyers became more interested in new technical developments.

11

Adapting Marketing Operations

Marketing costs and profit improvement

Three-quarters of the price paid by the housewife for a grocery product in a Western country is for the marketing effort involved in moving the product to her. Only one-quarter of the price — and in some fields much less than that — is the cost of making the product itself.

In 1850 the total marketing costs of the same product would have been 40%, not 75%. One of the effects of increasing competition is a disproportionate increase in marketing costs. Within the cost of the product, people pay for:

1 Widescale distribution, with many points of purchase located conveniently near to where they live.
2 Ready supply at short notice, with wide stockholding at various points along the distributive chain.
3 Heavy packaging costs, including inner wraps to protect the product, colourful packages, outer cartons for display on shelves, fibre cases for carrying, plus merchandising and sales aids to promote brands. This compares to the old days when grocery products were sold as bulk provisions displayed in open sacks of flour, salt, sugar and so on.
4 Direct advertising and sales promotion costs.
5 Heavy investment in new product research and development.
6 High sales costs, to the trade and out of it, to the consumer.

Hence the cost of marketing has been rising, not only because of inflation, but also in real terms because of increased competition . It should be stated however, that the relative cost of the total product to consumers, in terms of their purchasing power, has gone down equally remarkably as marketing costs have increased. Indeed, the advent of mass marketing techniques has made possible large scale production which has, to a large extent, created the economic wealth of the Western world. What we have really seen, therefore, is a grand switching of resources with a very much higher proportion of the total going into marketing and distribution areas while a much lower proportion has gone into production. The total offers an abundance of consumer wealth.

In itself, this is neither good nor bad, it is simply a fact which reflects the growing complexity of market demands, coupled with the increasing complexity of communication processes. What is true however, is that it is very difficult to see how to contain inflation of these marketing costs, let alone to reduce them. In a situation of full supply, any straight line cut in advertising or sales budgets will allow competitors to increase their sales volume. At a time of inflation, the problem in many markets is how to deescalate the total costs of marketing, while still retaining the economic benefits of free competition. During inflation one of the big advantages of being in a dominating market-leader situation lies in the extra flexibility for cost-cutting in marketing.

The problem within industrial marketing is identical, except that there is more emphasis on sales costs than upon advertising costs. The problem is slightly easier, in that the cost of marketing a product to industry is much lower, as a proportion of the total product cost, than in consumer marketing. Even so it is often a high proportion of the company's profits.

While it is very difficult to see how to apply major surgery to marketing costs, it is true that at the margin of expenditure there is generally room for savings without causing serious damage. It is equally true that the effect of inflation causes marketing costs to be directed to different channels. Clearly, a company opting for nil growth in the short term, can afford to reduce expenditure which would otherwise go to investment in new markets.

Three broad areas for profit improvement offer themselves:

1   An attack upon existing weaknesses in marketing planning and allocation, making the total more cost-effective.
2   A switch of funds in markets which are convoluted by changing demand and supply situations, by taking resources out of deteriorating markets and switching them into new market opportunities which develop.
3   Greater flexibility in marketing effort and the switch to a defensive marketing posture until new growth opportunities can be developed.

Market research

The marketing operation which is likely to substantially increase in real expenditure terms is market research. This has an extremely important role to play, in helping a business to counter inflation and in developing an effective profit improvement programme over the long term.

First, it must be used to identify the impact that rising inflation is likely to make upon a company's existing key markets. There are five possibilities:

The identification of latent demand. The pressures acting upon the market by rising costs and by product shortages, create latent demand situations where substantial bodies of customers share a strong need for products and services which do not at present exist. Particularly is this true of low cost materials and products which can be substituted for existing purchases and presented to the market as a means of assisting cost-cutting. The markets for simple cost-effective products with limited functions, will grow at the expense of high price sophisticated products.

The prediction of faltering demand, and of declining markets. Some markets, such as those for capital goods, are affected quickly and radically by inflation. Some sectors of all markets may gradually erode particularly at the margin of high price demand. Small market segments may disappear altogether as distributors and users carry out their own cost cutting programmes and rationalise their purchases. A wide range of product offerings may be reduced to fewer choices as a result of inflation. Research is required to identify this faltering demand so that new target markets can be selected.

The study of irregular demand, where the seasonal pattern of demand is subjected to fluctuation and departs from the normal timing pattern of supply. It is particularly important to identify markets which might become prone to government interference or disruption due to product shortages. Here research evidence is needed so that companies can plan ahead more carefully in order to build on any competitive advantage they may have, or to avoid sudden losses.

The assessment of full demand in a market, where the current level of supply is equal to the current level of demand. This is where a study of competitive factors is required, together with an assessment of the likely impact of inflation upon competition, customers, and supplies so that a reduced-cost defensive marketing strategy can be adopted.

The development of strategies to meet conditions of overfull demand, where the level of demand exceeds the supply. When product shortages occur, a study of the causes is vital since the total marketing operation must be altered. Salesmen will ration the product, prices may rise and the total marketing effort will be reduced. The degree to which a company operates this policy successfully will determine its long term reputation within the market. Research is vital in all aspects of buyer behaviour, competitive behaviour, and on the supply prospects, with the aim of determining the company strategy.

Company marketing operations in the past have suffered from three weaknesses in the area of information gathering. Within industrial marketing the absence of reliable market data relating to market sizes, market segments, growth trends and buying behaviour has often been woeful. Failure to examine markets in an orderly systematised fashion and on a continuous basis has caused many companies to suffer often massive losses as the markets change suddenly and without warning to the suppliers. Often this problem could be eased by better planning based upon reliable data.

The second great weakness, again within industrial marketing fields, although this is also experienced within consumer goods producers, is the failure to carry out adequate product tests. So many products are developed by management on a judgement basis and launched on to the market with little attempt to obtain an evaluation of the benefits and weaknesses to the customer. It is fully recognised that product testing of small samples is not generally possible within industrial markets, owing to the high original set up costs of tooling and jigging for small quantities, but the techniques of concept and attitudinal research within industry have advanced remarkably within the past five years, and reliable data relating to customers' likely attitudes and behaviour can now be obtained where once it would have been held to be purely theoretical. As product ranges become value analysed and sometimes degraded in quality, it is ever more critical to test out the basic assumptions within the market using formal research techniques. A relatively small investment at this stage can often rescue product change failures which would otherwise have disastrous repercussions upon profits.

Advertising and promotion

During inflation both the amount of money spent on advertising, its content and direction need to be reviewed. The marginal rates of advertising and promotional expenditure can be reexamined to see if a cutback has any appreciable effect. Much advertising expenditure is relatively unproductive. For example, the costs of advertising production are often well in excess of any creative benefits which are obtained. In fact, no one has yet established a sound correlation between high production and origination costs, and sound advertising which sells. If production costs could be shaved, the money could be directed into media channels to do its primary task, that of buying communications to the market. A contingency reserve is required in the sales promotion budget so that funds are available to exploit short range opportunities as they occur or to act defensively without the profit objectives being damaged.

Advertising funds require to be re-directed towards: products with reliable production and stable materials supply which are high profit contributors, and away from loss leading items. Defending the company against criticism relating to price changes or to product shortage, during rising inflation more corporate advertising of this kind is seen. Advertising assistance is needed to overcome resistance to price changes within customer groups. This is particularly important for the more tactical weapons of sales promotion which use market forcing techniques to soften the impact of price rises. Help could be given to end-users and customers to enable them to obtain more use from products which are in short supply. Sound corporate advertising campaigns explaining how to make the best use of scarce materials have considerable payoff in long term goodwill and customer acceptance. Customers could be assisted to overcome the problems which rising inflation causes. In the promotional area, several companies are pursuing a policy of customer development. In this kind of programme suppliers take the initiative with customers by carrying out end-user market surveys, providing technical advice and assistance, and often marketing advice where the customers are companies with limited management resources. This policy of providing 'self-help' schemes tends to maintain market stability and to build a loyal demand. The competitive edge it provides may be very considerable. Advertising and promotional themes could well concentrate more on explaining the functional advantages and benefits of products rather than appealing to other satisfactions. This would reflect a more rational approach in buying habits where price and performance are the main criteria.

Using the Systematic Approach

The use of the Systematic Approach in the marketing operations area will reveal a number of ideas for achieving the same ends but at lower cost. Various aspects of advertising and promotion plans need to be broken down into their component parts and then appraised to see if there are cheaper alternative ways of achieving the same or improved results. For example, a tendency to integrate advertising, promotion and personal selling effort has been observed among the major companies. The rapidly rising expenditure upon sports sponsorship and upon product publicity campaigns, for example, is seen in many countries of the world even though the sales results of such efforts cannot be measured. When a company already spends substantially on direct advertising it begins to question the marginal rate of return. The question is whether the final 10% of the advertising expense could not be better deployed in some other low-cost activity which would not replace advertising, but would substantially assist the selling approach. Those companies which have used say, press relations programmes to the technical press, know just how valuable such exercises can be, since the inquiries from editorial usually substantially outweigh the inquiries from direct advertising on a cost-for-cost basis.

A number of studies have been carried out to identify the source of buyer awareness or interest in new products. The results vary from industry to industry but, all sources agree that the two primary factors which influence the creation of awareness are, word-of-mouth from colleagues within the industry and editorial comments. The most significant factors at the clinching end of the sales process are personal selling and product demonstration.

The use of the Systematic Approach in covering these areas of company marketing operations will reveal many original and creative solutions to cost cutting problems.

Market planning

In many companies marketing planning procedures are very weak. Plans are often a series of programmes drawn up without specific objectives and are poorly integrated with the rest of the business. Such plans are, in effect, lists of the ways in which money is to be spent, without any attempt at evaluation of results even on a subjective basis.

The weaknesses in marketing planning procedures are:

1   A failure to make a thorough situation analysis supported by factual evidence drawn from data which exists outside the company, ie a too heavy reliance upon internal data.
2   A lack of clear objectives for each part of the programme, or objectives which are not time-dated and quantified.
3   Plans poorly integrated with other operations such as production or research and development, that is a failure of communications.
4   A failure to control the company operation according to the agreed plan, and failure to review results and adjust programmes.

Procedures in marketing planning follow several recognisable and discrete stages:

Situation Analysis. At this stage a description is required of the company's key markets and of the company's performance within them. This must make use of data generated about the market trends, and about competitive behaviour drawn from outside the company's own internal data. In marketing planning there is usually an over-abundance of internal data and far too little from outside.

Objective Setting. The objectives for the overall plan should be time-dated and quantified and should be based upon results. These can be sales volume, profit contribution, market share or distribution penetration. The objectives for the sub-plans such as sales organisation, advertising and promotion should also be results-oriented and measurable.

Strategy selection. This describes the broad methods by which the objectives will be met.

Tactical programmes. This describes the various integrated programmes which must be run and will indicate the actions to be taken, by whom, and when, for the plan to be carried out.

Control. During the course of operating the plan a series of review stages need to be built in so that key results can be analysed, new factors appraised and forward plans modified accordingly.

Marketing: overhead costs

The marketing management function can grow in a company to a point of diminishing returns, rather like product development. In a growth phase, the company will extend its personnel and services to invest in new market opportunities. In the early stages this is often very successful, after a product management structure has been built into the company. Nonetheless product managers have a tendency to trail other costs in their wake. When they are appointed they commission market research studies, institute packaging and product presentation changes, increase promotional budgets and add research and development work. For a company without such a management structure this can be very successful, with additional profits resulting from growth being more than enough to compensate for the additional overhead costs. During inflation however, particularly when a company makes plans based upon zero growth, it may be possible to reduce these overhead costs without damaging the marketing operation. Some costs must be maintained in order to exploit market opportunity when it occurs again and to handle day-to-day operations, but often these central management costs and services can be streamlined. Many marketing services for example, can be bought from outside specialists instead of being built in to company operations as fixed costs. This will make them more flexible and in that way they can be tailored to the company's seasonal peaks and troughs. It may also make them more accountable, in that the use of outside services tends to be continuously appraised. By comparison, internal staff services are seldom evaluated for their profit contribution. There may be some loss of effect however, since the outside organisation is divorced from the company's business and it may be more expensive in some cases to buy from outside. But the advantage of having a tightly run business with low fixed costs is very considerable during inflationary pressures, and marketing management should be reviewed along with the rest of general management for its cost effectiveness.

12

Improving Productivity in Sales and Distribution

A nil growth plan puts more demands upon the sales organisation, not less. The sales organisation required may be smaller and leaner but it must be of a higher quality necessary for flexible and more complex market demands.

Inflation puts a premium upon three aspects of sales organisation:

1 Adaptive sales strategies to handle product shortages and price changes.
2 Improvements in sales productivity.
3 Reduction of sales cost.

In a scarcity economy the role of selling is thought to decline. Selling is seen as a growth factor and one that seems to be important during periods of excess supply. However excessive demand puts as much strain on a sales organisation as excessive supply and a difficult mix of choices must be made to sell the available product in such a way as to maintain future market objectives.

Sales strategy during shortages

A sales organisation has two alternatives open to it during periods of temporary or permanent product shortage. The first is to attempt to reduce overall demand from all sources; the second is to selectively reduce demand, ie, from certain classes of customers.

Whatever strategy is selected for dealing with short supply situations, the salesman should make some effort to gain advantage from the extra market demand. For example, the company can insist upon customers meeting its credit terms promptly, or even moving to an early payment routine. The company may take the opportunity to reduce discounts, or to change from a high cost service pattern to a lower cost. In short supply situations, which are likely to be permanent, the company can reduce its sales costs, making fewer calls per customer, and so on.

The company can also attempt to change its customer mix, putting pressure upon the weaker, high cost customers, and concentrating upon its 'key' accounts. Although companies may be banned by law from showing customers favouritism during shortages, the decisions should be guided by long run profitability considerations and short term plans drawn up accordingly.

Allocation of product on proportional demand basis. This system has the advantage of being demonstrably logical and fair, although the sales force will still come under pressure from key customers for additional supplies and may have to hold some contingency reserve of product to deal with this situation. Where demand is highly variable, this system is impossible to administer.

Main supply to favourite customers, with remaining customers receiving a fraction of their requirements. This policy works only when it is backed by a longer term plan to deal with the time when full supply is available again. When the customer population is highly varied, with the company dependent upon a few large customers for the bulk of its profits, then this is the only reasonable strategy to adopt, despite the pressure it puts upon small customers.

Allocation on a highest bid basis. In this way those customers who are prepared to pay more, or to offer other advantageous terms, receive higher quantities. This technique may be banned by government legislation and has other long term risks attached to it when the product is in full supply again, for the company sacrifices any reputation it may have for fair trading in return for maximisation of short term profits. When the company is in a sole supply situation, or there is an industry wide agreement, perhaps unofficial, to practice a raising price technique then this may be the suitable strategy to select, particularly if the shortages will remain permanent. But the danger to company goodwill is clear, and the salesman must do his best to minimise the adverse reaction.

Rising inflation and the occurrence of shortages consequently provides a sales force with a new technique which involves the appearance of trying to discourage demand as a means of stimulating it. The technique of announcing a price rise in advance, or of giving the general impression that future supplies may be in short supply is one way of encouraging customers to buy more now.

To reduce the general level of demand involves using the full range of marketing operations techniques such as, reduction of sales promotion, cutting advertising, raising the price, and so on. The impact upon the personal selling task is to switch the sales effort to those products which are available and which may be regarded as substitutes for the product in short supply. The salesman's task in gathering information from the field is vital at this time, when customers are being exposed to offers from alternative sources of supply and trying out product substitutes. His task is to identify the changes in purchasing behaviour which occur during this stage and to foresee how demand will settle along new lines for the future.

The first-come, first-served basis. With a very wide customer population, where the selling process is close to order taking, this is often the only equitable way of handling temporary shortages caused by industrial disruption or by materials shortage. At this time salesmen will be put under considerable pressure from all categories of customer, particularly the larger ones will use every effort to exert leverage on the company supply situation.

Developing key customers

To erode unwelcome customers in the long term, the sales force has a number of opportunities which must be developed while the risk to the company's trade reputation is minimised. The salesman can discourage hope for future product availability and encourage customers to seek new suppliers of substitute products; they can avoid making sales calls on these customers; the company can provide poor service for them, long delivery lead times and so on and they find ways to generally make it difficult for these customers to receive product information.

During inflation, the handling of price changes to the customer is a permanent part of the salesman's task. The salesman must explain how costs have increased, show ways in which the company has reduced its costs to minimise the price increase, show what other cheaper substitutes are available from the company, and so on. The objective is to minimise the risk of buyers regarding the price increase as being either unfair or avoidable. Most buyers, most of the time, will grumble and carry on as before. The company which handles price changes in an overbearing manner however, without regard to the problems it poses for the customers, will cause more buyers to search for alternative sources of supply out of simple irritation.

During shortages, the salesman's counselling role is critical in showing how the use of the product can be altered to make it go further, by studying the customers problems to see where and how their problems can be eased, and by showing what alternatives are available. In this way, product shortages and price increases may be turned to a small advantage by enabling the salesman to develop key customers and to enhance goodwill by showing the trade that the company is sensitive to their problems and reasonable to deal with. He can also use the opportunity to negotiate longer term contracts, offer lower discounts and secure better payment terms. Inflation and shortage can undoubtedly present opportunities for enterprising companies.

Long term planning

For long term planning purposes the following questions need to be asked:

1   When is the company likely to face situations of product shortage either because of materials supply or, the disruption of production? How extensive are the situations likely to be?
2   How will competition attempt to reduce total demand, how do they allocate scarce products and how can the company gain a competitive or profitable advantage from this?
3   What role is played by sales management in deciding how such situations should be handled, and is the special difficulty of the personal selling task at this time recognised?
4   What are the implications of government policy and special legislation which may be prompted by company policies and which would damage either the market, the supply or long term company profitability?

The use of the Systematic Approach to sales and distribution

Within the sales operation the Systematic Approach technique to profit improvement can be used widely, in all areas of the sales operation. Every aspect of the company's sales and service operation and policy can be systematically reviewed with the purpose of improving the productivity of sales, developing profitable growth areas, and reducing cost.

How can sales volume be increased by 5% with a sales cost reduced by 5%?

A question such as this, modified to suit alternative company objectives will reveal ideas in the following areas:

1   Cutting the size of the sales force.
2   Changing sales methods.
3   Improving volume per order.
4   Increasing the order-to-call ratio.
5   Increasing price, reducing discounts.
6   Lowering customer service levels.
7   Concentration upon high-growth, high-profit customers.
8   Area expansion.
9   Reduction of customer population.
10   Change of sales force remuneration, incentives.
11   Identifying marginal opportunities for growth.
12   Improving sales skills, product, or customer knowledge.
13   Key account development.
14   Providing sales and customer incentives.

The range of possibilities is very wide indeed, once an examination of existing sales operations is undertaken. The really key aspects of the operation are:

The size and structure of the sales force. The productivity of sales per man in a small sales force is very high compared to the productivity of sales per man in a large sales force. This is because the smaller sales force is naturally concentrated more upon high volume accounts. Many high cost field sales forces can be reduced in size, if they are supplemented by alternative sales methods. For example, the use of the telephone in selling is growing very quickly throughout the Western world. Some sales forces organise their representatives to telephone smaller customers in each journey cycle instead of making a personal call upon them. If a visit is then required, they will make it while they are in the territory, otherwise they will leave the personal field visit until the next cycle. Other sales forces use a well trained telephone sales girl in the office to support four or five field salesmen. She can organise sales representatives appointments, identify customer prospects, offer customer incentive programmes and so on. Her role is to provide a basic level of service calls on the telephone to existing customer. She can, for example, offer new products. Her task in supporting the pioneering efforts of the field salesman is to obtain as much information about prospective customers as possible including the type of business, the types of products they use and the names of personnel who make buying decisions. In some cases she can attempt to sell them direct although her power to do so is very limited without support from the field. Even within technically intensive industries the use of a mixed telephone/field sales system has very considerable cost advantages. After all, one girl in the office can make up to fifty calls per day, compared to a field salesman making up to fifteen calls per day, even in highly clustered areas with simple sales tasks. Many industrial salesmen make about four calls per day or less. In this case there is a need to provide them with as much service support as possible to make their time more effective.

Identifying the marginal opportunities. However well controlled and well motivated a sales force it suffers from the problem that it could always do a little bit more or a little bit better if it tried. Given training the men could improve their closing techniques and convert more orders. They could plan their day a little better to squeeze in an extra call or two. They could make more pioneering calls to new customer prospects and make fewer service calls. They could improve the number of sales leads, and so on. This problem of sales force productivity goes right up the line to the sales director breaking into one more major account, or a regional manager opening up one new factor or wholesaler in a previously unsold area. The total sales organisation only needs a commitment to obtain these extra sales to make a considerable impact upon the total company sales volume. See figure 12.1. The opportunity for using the Systematic Approach down to individual sales territories and responsibilities should be taken using a question such as: 'If the total sales budget were to remain the same but you were to allocate it differently, what sales increases could you obtain, from where, and how?'

Increasing sales effectiveness – a case study

A company introduces a mixed sales force using telesales girls and fewer field salesmen. This can provide the same level of sales pressure with a 10% cut in sales costs, or the existing costs can be maintained which will provide an 11% increase in sales pressure. Which is the more profitable move? In Figure 12.1 the direct costs are 50%; the net profit is 10% and the sales cost is 10%. (A one-tenth reduction in sales cost converts to an 11% increase in sales potential.)

	Existing cost	Taking the savings	Increasing sales by 11%
Direct costs	50	50	55.5
Indirect costs	30	30	30
Sales cost	10	9	10
Net profit	10	11	15.5
Sales volume	100	100	111
Increase in net profit		+10%	+55.5%

Note: since we are increasing pressure at the margin of sales effectiveness, it would be unlikely that we can achieve the full 11% increase in sales. In a normal competitive market, the expected increase in sales volume might be more like 5%. In this case the increase in net profit would be 25%.

Figure 12.1   A comparison between cutting sales costs and increasing sales with existing costs.

Physical distribution

Physical distribution is a cost area, and purely a cost area of business. All that can be done by moving stuff is to harm it, – it can be aged, spoilt, broken, scratched, soiled, made stale, discoloured. The further it is moved and the more times it is handled, the more expensive it becomes. It can be finished, packaged in easy-to-carry loads, merely for others to steal it.

There are in effect no costs more resistant to pruning than distribution costs. If money is saved by cutting deliveries there will be an increase in vehicle size and stock holdings. If the vehicle is replaced less often, the repair costs go up. Cut the labour costs and the costs of automatic handling equipment go up; cut the supervision cost and the breakage cost rises. Cut out the pilfering in the warehouse, and the deals between loaders, despatchers, drivers and customers increase.

The costs of distribution and storage are spread erratically across several different budgets with no overall control. Finished goods storage is in the 'miscellaneous factory overhead' budget, packaging costs are in the materials budget, customer rejects are in the sales budget, order processing is in the production planning budget, delivery refusals are in the customer credits budget, and depot storage and transport is in the distribution budget. To say that physical distribution is the messiest and worst administered part of a normal manufacturing company's operation is a gross understatement.

The Systematic Approach to distribution

Physical distribution is one part of a business operation where use of the Systematic Approach looks attractive at first sight to improve efficiency but where there is a strong domino effect in that making a change for the better in one aspect of the operation, may cause a change for the worse in another. Instead, before the operation can be improved on a piecemeal basis, the entire distribution network must be examined. If after this total examination, the process looks efficient, then marginal savings can usually be found in most areas of the operation. For example:

1   Reducing distribution points.
2   Increasing central storage capacity.
3   Delivering less frequently.
4   Increasing automatic handling and order processing.
5   Cutting packaging and cartoning costs.
6   Less handling of fewer items.
7   Lower vehicle cost, repair costs, driver cost, petrol cost.

The usual problem in physical distribution is that at any one time, some goods are overstocked while others are understocked; some distribution points are located inconveniently for some markets; some customers receive a poor level of service, while others have a costly and rapid service available.

Often the distribution system is too complex or too inflexible. This results in people by-passing the normal system in order to provide customer service. Outdated locations for warehouses is another problem indicating that the nature and size of the business has changed over the years but the original distribution system has been retained. One of the most serious problems is that stocks are under the control of different people at various stages of the process. Raw materials under the purchasing department, goods in progress and finished under the production department, stocks awaiting delivery under sales department. None of this makes for efficiency, added to which, the calibre of distribution and transport management is often poor. The day cannot be foreseen when the transport manager's career path rises to chief executive in manufacturing organisations.

Distribution costs

There are two points of attack upon distribution costs. The first is upon the individual cost elements in the chain. The second is the manner in which these costs alter when changes in the system occur. For example, the total costs will change when the level of customer service is altered, or when the number of warehouses is changed. A cost-benefit analysis is required, covering every aspect of the chain. Starting with inbound transportation of materials and goods to the plant, their receipt, checking and handling, the analysis will include the management of finished stock, packaging, in-plant warehousing, bulk transportation, field warehousing, customer service, parts service, order processing and control. In addition, security, pilfering and breakage need attention. However, the effect of a change in total distribution procedure cannot be measured until the total cost of all the factors is known. Six opportunities for cost saving could be revealed:

1   The simplification of the total system, reducing depots or moving manufacturing nearer to the markets are examples.
2   Reduction in stocks. More frequent deliveries or concentration of stocks at fewer points will require lower balancing stocks.
3   Improvements in packaging. Smaller, more dense, standardised sizes provide greater efficiency in handling and storage.
4   More efficient methods and procedures, ie, handling procedures, order processing, transport methods might be improved.
5   Technical improvements. Regarding materials handling and transport there have been a number of new products and innovations in recent years to speed the flow of goods at reduced cost.
6   Channels of distribution. Alternative methods of reaching the end users of the product might be found through the selection of alternative trading channels.

While inflation and product shortages cause the movement of goods to be highly uncertain; indeed, temporary shortages of product are often caused by industrial action within the distribution system itself, the need is for high flexibility and for alternative distribution routes to the market to be made available at short notice. When industrial crisis occurs either within the market or within the company, the impact is witnessed visibly within distribution. It is in depots bereft of stock and totally cleared that one sees the effect of demand exceeding the supply of goods. Equally it is when depots are filled to the brim with cartons and containers when that the problem of distribution disruption can be seen.

13

Pricing Strategy during Inflation

In the long run, inflation may be seen to have been very good for some companies. First it will teach companies how to conserve their resources and improve their efficiency in a situation of near zero growth, rather than allowing waste to build up in untrammelled expansion. Second, it will promote pricing strategy to its proper position in managements' scale of values: at the top. Research evidence shows that most companies hold their pricing policy well down their list of priorities, well below product quality, research and development, and their marketing and sales operations. In times of growing material shortage and when markets are disturbed by inflation this will slowly change. Buyers will become more important than salesmen, research and development will turn inwards to improve the profitability of the product range instead of widening it, and companies will concentrate on the value of their price/quality offering to the market. Buyers will focus less and less upon non-price factors.

This suggests a change of emphasis rather than a complete alteration in buyer behaviour. Advertising will still make appeals to emotional responses, buyers will still react to persuasion, but the focus of the buyer/seller relationship will be on more rational factors such as value for money. Planning a future pricing policy during continuous inflation is vital. Without a plan, companies are at the mercy of every whisper of change in costs, watching their profits erode until finally they must raise their prices in order to survive, whether or not they are in a suitable market position. Inflation will run the business. To bring it under control means tackling first the very difficult question of the relationship of their price levels to cost inflation over a period of time. Figure 13.1 shows

		5% sales volume lost	Inflation increased by 5%	Then offer 5% discount to meet competition
Net sales	100	95	95	90.25
Direct costs	50	47.5	91.875	91.875
Overheads	40	40		
Net profit	10	7.5	3.125	(1.625 loss)
% change against profit		−25%	−69%	−116%

There are thousands of companies making this mistake today. In itself the loss of 5% sales volume does not seem much. Also many companies are finding their prices lagging behind inflation, and a 5% difference does not seem large. Many companies are trying to buy back sales volume in declining markets by giving away extra discounts 'because they must meet competition'. The cumulative effect of these changes is disastrous.

Figure 13.1   How to make losses easily.

how inflation and a slight fall in turnover can destroy profits, if a company has no pricing plan.

   Without a pricing plan, companies short of scarce materials will be willing to pay prices well above those they can afford for essential supplies, hoping to recover the costs from price increases. Sooner or later their end markets will turn to substitute products, or price legislation from governments will restrict them. Companies in the happier position of dominating their markets, or those with access to essential materials will wish to raise prices to the level the market can bear, forcing more government interference, creating further inflation and disturbance in their end markets. By this process, if conditions of shortage grow to acute levels, they could end by destroying the capitalist system itself, preceded by economic collapse and social unrest. The need for a pricing plan for individual companies is clear. In the case of the producers of essential materials, the case for industry-wide collaboration on pricing policies designed to serve the social needs of people is also clear, despite the dangers of unhealthy side effects such as market-rigging and the creation of cartels. Whether the companies involved in such industries will be prepared to forgo the attractive and profitable technique of demanding what the market will bear is another matter. As Western societies move more towards the social democratic left with more government interference and wider public participation in what was previously the private sector of industry, there is no certainty that the free enterprise system will survive. Meanwhile an individual company's objective will be served best by building a pricing strategy into its corporate plan.

Pricing strategy for the individual company

A company's pricing strategy involves taking the view that its rate of price increases over time will be in general:

1   Lower than the anticipated level of cost inflation.
2   At the anticipated level of cost inflation.
3   Above the anticipated level of cost inflation.

The effect of any government regulations on price will simply close off some of these options to varying degrees, restraining companies from adopting the higher-than-inflation pricing strategy. Government pricing regulations will not absolve companies from the need to make a pricing plan, they will make it more necessary through adding one further factor to build into the model.

A pricing plan must take into account a company's freedom to act within the framework of the following factors:

1   The dominance of the company's market position; a company's market leverage on prices moves directly in line with its share of the market.
2   The degree to which substitute products are available; the more distinct and necessary a product, the more pricing leverage can be exerted.
3   The likelihood of competitive response.
4   The anticipated rise in costs.
5   The price elasticity of demand. The degree to which sales and price are related within the chosen market sector. Some markets, notably those involving fashion and taste considerations, sometimes have an inverse demand curve where sales may actually rise in line with higher comparative prices until an upper threshold of demand is met. In most markets an inverse demand curve operates at the lowest level of quality and price offered.
6   The company's long term business and market objective.
7   The anticipated developments in technology which may bear upon future production costs.
8   The need for company growth in sales volume.
9   Government restrictions on price.
10   The company's short term profit requirement.
11   Relatively small pricing moves which may have a dramatic impact upon profits.

A pricing strategy for inflation

Clearly the pricing strategy adopted for one company will be totally different from the strategy adopted by another company, even within the same field. One possible strategy is outlined below:

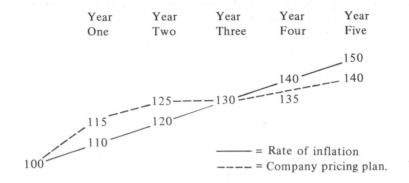

Figure 13.2   A pricing strategy to cover inflation: a theoretical model

This company chooses a long term objective to achieve a low price market position by year five, well supported by product quality and service. To do this they maximise short-term profits through taking price increases up to the rate of cost inflation, and by changing their product mix to force the sales of high margin lines. This has the effect of moving their price levels above the rate of cost inflation, and they then set about a continuous profit improvement programme. They concentrate upon their strengths, profit strip their weak areas and avoid investment in growth in the first two years. They plough back their profits into increasing the efficiencies of their business.

They use their high profit position at the end of year two to hold prices below the level of the market. With the returns from the profit improvement programme still flowing in year three they continue to trade at a price lower than competition, giving them a strong market edge and a superior contingency reserve at year five. They use a pricing plan based upon the recognition that relatively small differences in price have remarkable effects upon profits and that a low price market strategy must be sustained by efficiency.

In this case the company's long term objective is to arrive at a suitable market position in five years time which will provide it with a sound contingency reserve in case of financial trouble, or alternatively, will enable it to move into an aggressive market position against competition. The company chooses to limit the growth of its output and to maximise its short term profit position. It therefore takes all the price increases allowed under pricing regulations wherever it can without damaging its markets. It drops loss making products, boosts high margin lines and takes every possible action to raise the level of its gross margin. This has the effect of moving its general level of prices up above the level of cost inflation.

Assuming the policy is successful, this provides the company with the necessary short term funds which are then deployed in making the business more efficient (rather than for growth investment). By year three the company should be in a position to exploit its more favourable profit base and can then reinvest in market development with a pricing plan based upon lower-than-inflation increases. This gives it a strong competitive advantage, backed by funds to exploit this in the market place.

The advantage of a drive for short term profit improvements, reinvested in further efficiency before expanding sales, is clear, and the company has retained control over its affairs. It has taken five years for it to contain inflation and this is the time scale that is necessary for planning.

If government pricing constraints make the early part of this strategy impossible, then the alternative is to take as much price increase as is allowed, while reducing the level of customer service and lowering product quality as far as management dares. No one suggests that this is a risk-free policy, although there are ways to minimise the risks. But doing nothing at all about inflation is a greater risk, and the very process of preparing a pricing plan will uncover profit opportunities which were not previously seen.

The Systematic Approach to pricing

Using the Systematic Approach in the area of short term pricing opportunities identifies a wide number of pricing/quality alternatives. The question will be: 'How can we obtain a 5% increase in our net selling price, without affecting sales volume?'

Some answers will be:

1   Alter the basis of the pricing method.
2   Change the discount structure.
3   Raise the prices of small selling lines and uneconomic products.
4   Charge for special service.
5   Build inflation escalation clauses into price contracts.

The ideas will speedily move into the quality of product and service offered, since pricing is so completely identified with the rest of the company's quality offering hence:

1   Drop the product and replace it with one high price/high quality and one low price/low quality version.
2   Reduce the costs of packaging/quality control/materials etc.
3   Reduce the costs of transport/stocking/order processing, and so on, into the costs of the business itself.

Notice that some of these suggestions such as, dropping the product and replacing it with high and low price versions, or reducing the quality of non functional features such as packaging and service will overcome many government pricing restrictions. When government pricing legislation is directed at limiting the company's net profit margin rate, in addition to restraining prices, then the available moves for the company are reduced further though options are still open. Whatever price or margin restrictions are exerted, history shows that companies will find ways to evade them whenever their survival is threatened.

Meeting price competition

A peculiar phenomenon of inflation is that it encourages price wars. Although prices are generally going up, some companies move up their prices below the rate of competition's increase thereby hoping for a sales advantage. The price war is often seen in the discount offerings made to and encouraged by the trade. Control over discounts and a valid discount policy is vital during inflation, for a number of reasons:

1   Discounts may fall within pricing regulations as they do in the British Price Code.
2   It is generally harder to reduce a customer's discounts than it is to increase the list price.
3   Buyers seek more favourable discount terms when prices go up and play off one supplier against another.
4   Additional discounts tend to stay in the customer's pocket rather being passed through to the end user, hence the market size is not increased.
5   Short term and promotional discounts have a tendency to become firmly established as standard discounts.
6   Standard discounts for bulk orders or for rapid payments or for turnover volume have a tendency to be claimed, even when the conditions under which they are offered are not met.

The case for variable discounts negotiated separately with each customer is very strong; if possible the discount arrangement should be specific over a distinct period of time or over a particular delivery or order. This allows the supplying company to re-negotiate, providing room for bargaining.

There is also the paradox that while many, if not most, customers will want to negotiate the best terms they can get, the fact is that many companies find that purchasing routines are often inert or that their salesmen can often negotiate a lower discount successfully than would be otherwise offered. Industry practice on this varies and it may be impossible for a supplier to vary his terms against his competition; equally it would be foolish for suppliers not to take advantage of slack buying where they can, without threatening their sales volume.

One of the ways of meeting price competition is to radically alter the pricing policy away from that of competition. For example, customers can be offered:

1 A lower price, and pay a charge for delivery or for after sales service.
2 Lower prices for bulk orders delivered less frequently.
3 Lower prices against a guaranteed order over time, paid in advance, or in stages.
4 Lower prices for sole supplier rights.
5 Reciprocal deals, with products and services being exchanged.

Figure 13.3 (p.134) tabulates the increased revenue which must result from a straight price cut, simply to break even.

The combinations of price offerings are many, and using the Systematic Approach a number of ingenious pricing solutions have emerged. In general, if a customer can be shown that his purchasing pattern can be altered to conform to the efficiency of the supplier company, and if this can be done on a wide-scale basis across enough customers, the resulting savings – or part of them at least – can be passed on.

There are two ways of negotiating prices apart from demonstrating product quality. The first is to reveal to the customer how he can arrange his purchasing and payment pattern in such a way as to show savings to the supplier; the second is to demonstrate how a higher priced offering can be made more cost effective to the customer by allowing him to make savings on his own costs.

Making price changes

The way in which companies announce price changes to the market is critical. With a price increase, the principle is to avoid disturbing or irritating the market as far as possible. With a price reduction or an increased discount, the principle is to promote the move vigorously.

A series of increases can be built into the pricing plan at predetermined intervals. These need not be implemented if competitive or inflationary conditions make it unwise, but at least the action should be prepared as a contingency. To cover an inflation rate of 10% per annum may require two increases of just over 5½%, one in the first half of the year and another in the second half. During inflation, buyers are receiving news of price increases from a wide range of suppliers all the time. They cannot change their suppliers and search around for a new one every time there is a price change so most of the increases will be accepted, with resistance perhaps, but it will be seen that the process is inevitable. Indeed, they will have budgeted for increases, possibly unknown to the salesman. The important thing is not to draw attention to the company's price increase since this may cause the buyer to search for a new

Price cut	5%	10%	15%	20%	25%	30%	35%	40%	45%	50%
1%	25.0%	11.1%	7.1%	5.3%	4.2%	3.4%	2.9%	2.6%	2.3%	2.0%
2	66.6	25.0	15.4	11.1	8.7	7.1	6.1	5.3	4.7	4.2
3	150.0	42.8	25.0	17.6	13.6	11.1	9.4	8.1	7.1	6.4
4	400.0	66.6	36.4	25.0	19.0	15.4	12.9	11.1	9.8	8.7
5	—	100.0	50.0	33.3	25.0	20.0	16.7	14.3	12.5	11.1
6	—	150.0	66.7	42.9	31.6	25.0	20.7	17.6	15.4	13.6
7	—	233.3	87.5	53.8	38.9	30.4	25.0	21.2	18.5	16.3
8	—	400.0	114.3	66.7	47.1	36.4	29.6	25.0	21.6	19.0
9	—	1000.0	150.0	81.8	56.3	42.9	34.6	29.0	25.0	22.0
10	—	—	200.0	100.0	66.7	50.0	40.0	33.3	28.6	25.0
11	—	—	275.0	122.2	78.6	57.9	45.8	37.9	32.4	28.2
12	—	—	400.0	150.0	92.3	66.7	52.2	42.9	36.4	31.6
13	—	—	650.0	185.7	108.3	76.5	59.1	48.1	40.7	35.1
14	—	—	1400.0	233.3	127.3	87.5	66.7	53.8	45.2	38.9
15	—	—	—	300.0	150.0	100.0	75.0	60.0	50.0	42.9
16	—	—	—	400.0	177.8	114.3	84.2	66.7	55.2	47.1
17	—	—	—	566.7	212.5	130.8	94.4	73.9	60.7	52.6
18	—	—	—	900.0	257.1	150.0	105.9	81.8	66.7	56.3
19	—	—	—	1900.0	316.7	172.7	118.8	90.5	70.1	61.3
20	—	—	—	—	400.0	200.0	133.3	100.0	80.0	66.7
21	—	—	—	—	525.0	233.3	150.0	110.5	87.7	72.5
22	—	—	—	—	733.3	275.0	169.2	122.2	95.7	78.7
23	—	—	—	—	1115.0	328.6	191.7	135.3	104.6	85.5
24	—	—	—	—	2400.0	400.0	218.2	150.0	114.3	92.6
25	—	—	—	—	—	500.0	250.0	166.7	125.0	100.0

At intersection of price cut row and current gross profit column find percentage increase in unit sales required to maintain the same absolute gross profit as before the price cut.

Note: Remember your net profit will go down as you must transport, store, and finance higher unit volumes.

supplier out of exasperation. The rules are:

1 Raise prices when everyone else does, if possible.
2 Avoid too frequent price rises.
3 Provide a short moratorium on the price increase for key customers.
4 Provide advance notice of the price increase allowing customers to stock up at old prices.
5 Offer some economy at the same time – a price reduction on small selling items – a promotional short term discount, and so on.
6 Make a good case for the price increase. Explain the cost increases causing the lift in price, and also demonstrate how the company's productivity or profit improvement programme has helped to absorb some of the increase.
7 Show customers how they can change their buying pattern to minimise the effect of the increase.
8 Introduce a new lower price, lower quality version of the product.
9 Offer alternative payment or service terms.

On the other hand a price reduction has mostly inverse rules:

1 Cut the price when the competition is quiet, or preferably when they are raising their prices.
2 Make the price cut deep enough, in most fields a 15% cut is required to make the market shift. It has to be deep enough to overcome the normal inertia of the market and to 'pay' a buyer for his trouble in considering a new supplier.
3 Do it without notice and promote it very widely. Be careful not to stock load large customers before-hand.
4 Do it only when the price cut can be sustained for a long time, preferably when competition will have great difficulty in meeting it.
5 *Never* do it unless the market is demonstrably price sensitive.
6 *Never* do it as a crisis measure when profits are low and the market is turning down, competitors will copy to survive, and a price or discount war will result.
7 Do it on selected loss leading lines, with other products trailed at normal prices.

Part 3

ACTION PROGRAMMES FOR PROFIT IMPROVEMENT

14

Action Steps to Implement the Systematic Approach to Profit Improvement

The Systematic Approach to Profit Improvement does not need specialised management knowledge or a management consultant to implement it. It can be carried through by experienced general managements in companies large and small, in service or manufacturing industries, with a wide product range sold to a mass of customers, or to a single product company servicing one main customer. It acts primarily as a change agent; that is, it's main value lies in convincing the company management at all levels that something must be done to improve profits. It secures their active cooperation and participation and provides a focus for their profit improvement efforts. Carried through at all management levels of the company, it provides a systematic view of all areas of the company operation by those in charge and those primarily affected. It makes staff conscious of the need for making profits and for saving costs at every level of the enterprise.

Preliminary general management considerations

The causes of the problem: the decision to install a profit improvement programme will be determined by the nature of the problem facing the company. The spectrum of problems range from sudden crisis when a series of one-shot cost savings are required, to a need for the company to take action to avoid inflation and to generate growth in the future. In this latter case, a continuous profit improvement programme is required to tighten up the efficiency of the enterprise. The causes of the problem need to be identified together with their likely impact upon the future profits of the business. This will determine the style of programme to institute, the size and nature of the objectives, and the timing schedule for results.

Deciding upon the approach: there are some aspects of an enterprise which Senior Management alone can determine, and there are two alternative styles of approach which can be used for the implementation of the programme. Senior management must determine beforehand the questions which relate to general organisation structure, particularly divisional responsibilities. They must also determine the broad outline of pricing strategy to cope with the inflation. It is they who must also calculate the overall objectives for the profit improvement programme and the time by which they should be reached. Each of these questions may need to be studied by specialists but at policy level they are not suitable for opening up to other levels of management for discussion and review. Once the policy lines are cleared, however, then these questions can be broken down into sub-functions and other levels of management can then participate. The general principle is never to give a man the task of deciding the role and functions of himself and of his colleagues, certainly never to ask him to discuss his superiors situation but to focus his attention on his subordinate levels of authority.

The next stage is to determine whether the profit improvement programme will be handled and carried through by one team of full time specialists, called a Profit Improvement Team and working from department to department to identify and implement changes, or whether a full Systematic Approach should be used to involve the cooperation of management in general, under the guidance of a full time controller of the projects. The first method, using the specialist approach, works well if the aim is gradually to improve the efficiency of the business. The full Systematic Approach however, produces a greater range of savings more quickly and is required for emergency situations.

Creating the conditions for change: during a financial crisis, managers and staff may be nervous and worried about their personal situations. The prospect of change of any kind creates tension among those likely to be affected. These underlying fears must be resolved by showing the staff the problem, its cause, and how the company might be affected. The next stage is to obtain their commitment to assisting in the change, working with the programme and in helping to create the right climate of opinion within the organisation. The principles are to explain the facts, discuss the problem openly, invite management participation to create solutions to the problems, communicate the news about the progress and results of the programme, and to welcome feedback information and new ideas.

Implementing the systematic approach

Calling the initial meeting: the initial meeting which may last one full day needs serious preparation beforehand. Strictly, it is an in-company seminar. Its purpose is to explain the problem facing the company and to trace its likely effect in the future; to demonstrate to management how relatively minor changes in sales, costs, and prices have a large impact on company profits; to set up a broad objective for the Profit Improvement Programme; and to generate the first clutch of ideas. The number of people present should not be too many – about 12 to 16 – with the most senior managers being provided with a short personal briefing about the purpose of the meeting beforehand. The meeting is asked to study the style of the presentation since they may be asked to carry out the same Systematic Approach within their own divisions and down the line.

The meeting

The presenter should give a prepared outline of the overall problem, preferably using an overhead projector, which will also be useful later. He should then go on to show the essential parts of the Systematic Approach possibly making use of the kinds of models described in this book, such as the effect of small changes in sales, costs and prices upon profits and the problem of finding the interactive savings between departments. He should supplement these with short examples of cost efficiency shown by the organisation in the past and invite other examples to be quoted from the audience. He should explain the problems of change causing tension in the organisation and the importance of creating the right climate of opinion by openness and by inviting participation which should be encouraged down the line.

Generating ideas The presenter should then set up the first 'double bind' problem such as:

'IF WE HAD TO IMPROVE PROFITS BY £ . . . . . (SAY, 50%) WITHOUT RESORTING TO PRICE CHANGES, WRITE DOWN SIX WAYS IN WHICH YOU BELIEVE THIS MIGHT BE DONE.'

This first exercise requires the audience to work privately for ten minutes or so in thinking about the business as a whole, not only their own functions. The presenter should explain that the problem is purely theoretical at this stage, without any time limit set for the required profit increase, and its purpose is to obtain some ideas for discussion. The presenter then asks for a few ideas to be quoted to him at random, these he records on the screen without comment or discussion. The selected ideas should be specific and practical such as 'introducing value analysis to the product range' rather than general and unspecific such as 'becoming more efficient in production' or 'selling more'. These general ideas need to be broken down into specific suggestions by the presenter asking the question, 'How?'. Equally, some suggestions may be too narrow and small, these can be opened up into broader ideas by asking the question 'Why?'. At this stage there is no evaluation and no discussion of the ideas which should be roughly clustered on the screen into the divisional areas such as 'production', 'sales', 'finance' and so on. When twenty or thirty ideas — good and bad — have been recorded the next stage begins.

Preliminary discussion: each idea now needs to be very roughly evaluated for its likely contribution to additional profit in a full-going year and the time by which this might be achieved (after the idea has earned back any extra cost it has incurred in the setting-up phase). The original proposer is asked for his rough assessment, even his guess will be sufficient at this stage and this is recorded on the screen. Some argument will be caused among the other members of the audience on grounds of practicability, timing and profit estimates, this should be allowed for a short time but not to the point of heated debate. Again the purpose should be explained, the intention is to create ideas merely as food for thought and to widen discussion generally, not to select projects.

After this preliminary evaluation some ideas will seem more practical than others, some ideas will be too costly or risky, some will produce little additional profit in relation to the work they entail.

Preliminary selection of ideas: finally, the general discussion is closed down, and the audience are asked once again to write down six ideas which, in the light of the discussions they have heard or new ideas which have been prompted during the discussion, now seem to them to be most practical and worthwhile to develop into projects. The lists of these suggestions are collected and a private assessment can now be made by general management of those projects which, in their view, and in the view of their managers, are the most feasible. The final selection of projects should not be made necessarily upon the basis of those collecting the most votes — these are often the ideas which are going to be the most difficult to carry through — but the general lines of direction for profit improvement projects can now be determined.

Some ideas will be simple and their implementation will rest with functional managers who can be operate them within existing budgets. The managers in charge of these functions can then be asked to carry them through with their own staff, also involving the management of any other departments which may be affected. The other ideas now need to be turned over to project teams.

The projects

The projects control team: one small Control Team led by a member of senior management needs to be set up to implement and control the efforts of all the project teams carrying through the profit improvement programme. This senior group assesses the projects and plans, determines the general objectives for each, recruits the leaders of project teams, reviews progress, secures the necessary resources for the project teams, communicates information and assesses results. Its task is to oversee the rest of the work and to supply the motivation and drive. Its primary function after the setting-up of individual project groups is progress chasing and control. The members should be chosen for their personal qualities in supplying drive and energy and they should be acceptable to, and trusted by, the project teams with whom they must work. In a large diffuse organisation, a senior Profit Improvement Team may need to be set up at the head of each divisional function. In a small organisation the responsibility might rest with one senior executive who acts as overall Projects Controller. But the position should be a full-time one, at least during the setting-up and implementation phases of the programmes. Otherwise the initiative will be lost, the energy to see projects through will erode and the benefits from the initial meeting will be washed out.

To examine a project the ten key questions about company activity listed in chapter five (p. 44) on General Management can generally be asked.

The phases in a project. There are seven distinct phases in developing a project, each one of which must be thoroughly completed before proceeding to the next:

Information phase. To obtain the essential facts relating to the project; to define the project and its objectives and to relate these to the cost and risk of achieving them.

Speculation phase. To produce as many alternative ideas as possible for reaching the desired objective within the framework of the project. The full Systematic Approach may be useful at this point with some open ended projects; but any idea generation and creative technique may be applied.

Evaluation phase. The determination of which are the best ideas, their costs, the problems of developing and implementing them and their feasibility.

Planning phase. The construction of a work plan for converting the ideas into tangible proposals together with a timing schedule. Here a network analysis may be required

The Report phase. The preparation and submission of planned proposals to general management and to the line managements involved.

Execution phase. In carrying out the plans, the entire problem solving process may need to be repeated from time to time as difficulties occur.

Review phase. The review of the project and its results, once it has been completed and installed. This determines better methods, and provides experience for subsequent projects.

Controlling the projects Each team will have its own ideas about how to deal with its projects and the problem solving techniques to use. It is important that answers should not be pursued in development either before the objective for the project team has been agreed or before all the information is obtained. A monthly progress report showing projects completed, new projects started, and noting progress on existing projects should be issued, together with estimates of savings and subsequently the realised savings, if these can be calculated and set against estimates. A monthly review of all the project teams progress, conducted by the Project Controller, is essential.

The full-time profit improvement team

The purpose of a full-time Profit Improvement Team is to work with each department in turn to produce greater efficiency and profit. The Team members should be composed of mobile executives with a variety of functional experience, chosen because of their previous line or staff management successes and not necessarily on grounds of seniority. A small team of young and successful middle managers covering finance, technical production and marketing is typical.

Where to use it The Team should be used in departments or in subsidiary companies where a high leverage is exerted upon profits. A company selling high material cost products will apply it in purchasing, another with a high delivery cost will apply it in distribution, and so on. The team works with supervisors, first line managers, middle and senior management, acting as an internal consultant group. Their task is to identify which activities and operations can be discontinued or streamlined and how it should be done within the existing management capabilities.

The steps to be taken. The internal Profit Improvement Team carries out the following activity in concert with departmental management:

Pre-study activity — first line management is asked to prepare an activity study or review of the work of the department based upon the hours worked and an assessment of the quality of this work. To formulate plans it may be helpful to compare the work done with the job specifications of the personnel employed.

Preliminary interviews — these are held with the existing management team in order to develop profit improvement ideas, contributions coming from both sides.

Development of ideas — these are worked on in the normal way in order to challenge activities to see if a combination of ideas or activities will help, or to streamline the process.

Check lists — a Profit Improvement Team regularly confronted with similar problems is likely to acquire the habit of working through the solutions by a series of systematised steps. The use of specialised check lists is invaluable to those who are examining operations where the actions to be determined are repetitive, or where the problem is unfamiliar. The cockpit drill which pilots use before take-off is a good example of actions which are diverse but repetitive and where the check list procedure is useful.

Profit improvement recommendations — these are then made to the management of the function which has the task of carrying them through, and making them work.

Communications

Communication of progress. The need for a sound company communications programme throughout the work of a profit improvement programme is very strong. This must operate at two levels and be a two-way process:

1 Two-way Communication of Information.
2 Two-way Communication for Action.

For information purposes, the company management and staff at all levels need to know of the purpose of the Profit Improvement Programme, who is running it, how it might affect their departments, and what help is required from them. It is important that staff recognise that the Profit Improvement Programme has the full backing of senior management. Also for information purposes, management and staff need to know of the progress of work, and any results achieved during the course of the Programme. As projects are completed, and as new ones are set up, they should be asked for their contributions in terms of ideas and suggestions for improvement. Successful ideas and their sponsors should be recognised.

For action purposes, communications are required to see that instructions are carried out, to note when tasks have been completed and to exchange essential information between the active members of the group in order to develop the work. For this purpose, verbal and visual communications media, through formal discussions and reviews, to exchange and compare notes, is more important than the written word which should be used to confirm decisions and to implement the next stages of action. The fullest possible use should be made of visual aid material since some kinds of information can be communicated sensibly only by drawing it and seeing it. Statistical information needs reinforcement through models and charts to make it comprehensible. Samples of visual methods of communications data are shown in Figure 14.1. This is critically important during the development stage of projects so that everyone understands fully the implications of the data.

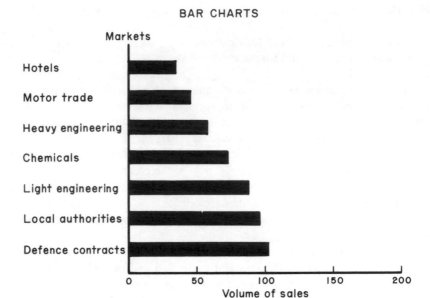

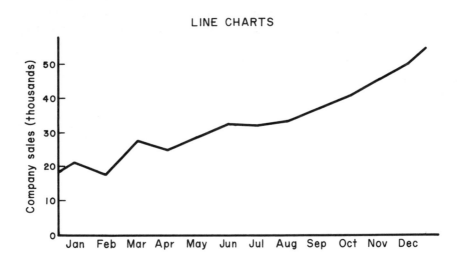

Figure 14.1   **Visual communication of data**

Figure 14.1 Continued

MULTIPLE BAR

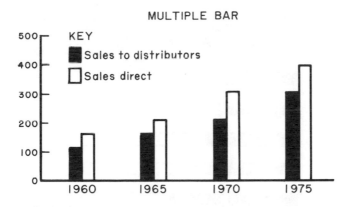

TWO-DIRECTION LINE CHART

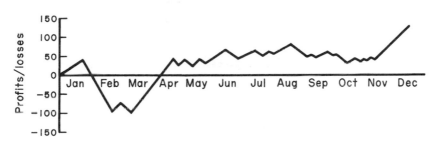

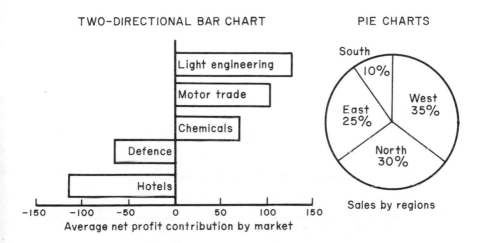

TWO-DIRECTIONAL BAR CHART

Light engineering

Motor trade

Chemicals

Defence

Hotels

−150 −100 −50 0 50 100 150
Average net profit contribution by market

PIE CHARTS

Sales by regions

Figure 14.1   Continued

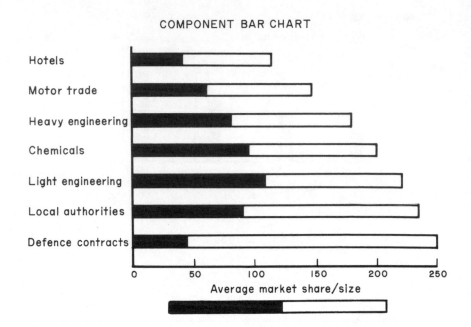

COMPONENT BAR CHART

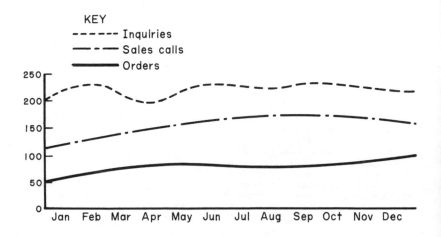

MULTIPLE LINE

15

Checklist for Profit Improvement Ideas

The approach:

Look for simultaneous but small changes in costs, sales volume and price.
Look for savings in the interactive costs between departments.
Largest savings are gained only in the long term.
Watch the risk to the future of cutting costs today.
Substantial short term savings can come only from surgical operations.
Concentrate on high-cost areas where substantial savings are to be found.
Examine long standing practices, habits, routines, organisations.

General management:

Cut salaries and indirect wages.
Cut running expenses.
Cut fixed costs.
Change the organisation structure.
Change the management system and routine.
Produce integrated long-term and short-term plans.
Use sources of outside data as well as internal company figures.
Evaluate management effectiveness.
Install tight budgeting: to cut marginal expenses
  to promote marginal opportunities
  to make interactive savings.
Install the tight budgeting sequence throughout the company at all levels.

Install a management audit to appraise: the information.

the system and control procedures

the organisation structure

the technical and management competence

Buy services from outside: research, product development, data processing, accounting, graphics, promotion, sales support, public relations, library information, market statistics, personnel, advertising, etc.

Pricing

Plan pricing policy to cover inflation over future years.

Alter pricing methods.

Reduce discounts.

Alter discount structure and method.

Tighten up discount procedure and policy.

Raise prices of small/uneconomic lines.

Charge for services.

Build inflation clauses into contracts and estimates.

Make price changes to minimise buyer irritation: make out a good case, offer a reduction or extra service at the same time, provide advance notice, raise prices at the same time as competition, show customers how they can reduce costs.

Note Some of these actions and others suggested may fall within the framework of government legislation on Pricing.

Financial accounting:

Correct accounts for inflation; watch machinery depreciation, stock valuations, land and property valuations, the value of borrowings.

Negotiate better credit terms through purchasing department.

Delay payment to creditors.

Pursue overdue accounts through better control, better communications.

Negotiate terms of business strictly through sales calling on debtors' bought ledger departments and financial controllers.

Speed up cash management by stage payments, rapid banking, flexible sources of finance, fast invoicing.

Improve security.

Cut departmental salaries and wages.

Cut departmental expenses.

Cut departmental fixed costs.

Reduce capital base through use of flexible assets, leasing, bought-out services.

Management accounting:

Replace historical accounting with standard costing.
Question established rule of thumb allocations.
Use more flexible costing approach.
Break down variances further.
Faster reconciliation with financial accounts.
Cost products and product groups down to net profit.
Cost control materials: identify wastage, rejects, breakages.
Allocate factory indirect costs to products.
Alter stock valuation standards and correct for inflation.
Set labour cost standards closer to realised costs than to ideal.
Identify highly productive labour costs.
Alter transfer pricing systems.
Introduce cost accountant to: purchasing department.
    marketing department.
Cost the following to net profit: large orders
    customers
    markets
    depots
    sales areas.

Purchasing:

Identify the company's purchasing Decision Making Unit, examine for weak-
    nesses.
Examine over-specification.
Improve supplier search and evaluation procedure.
Promote purchasing function to contribute to management decisions.
Apply a weighting system to purchases: Degree of essentiality of product
    Level of risk in purchase
    Proportionate cost against total purchases.
Apply a continuous evaluation of offers.
Concentrate upon the high value materials and components.
Apply regular stock checks.
Apply better quality control on goods inward.
Survey existing suppliers for cost reduction ideas.
Take discounts for prompt payment.
Negotiate new terms.
Alter product design to allow for standard parts purchasing.
Improve stock control and re-ordering system.
Involve purchasing in product elimination decisions.
Place guaranteed orders in exchange for bulk prices.

Improve supplier evaluation for: failure prevention costs.
    accident costs.
    level of service.
    accuracy.
Use supplier development techniques: in key materials areas.
    in high costs areas.
    in situations of doubtful supply.
    for unusual demands
    for too distant suppliers
    for non-standard parts
    for excess production capacity.
When materials are in short supply consider techniques of purchasing: coercion
    inducement
    education
    persuasion.

Production:

Check tolerances in specifications and widen.
Check quality control limits and widen.
Limit disruption to work flow.
Reduce prime costs.
Introduce value analysis to examine 'use' and 'cost' values.
Introduce value analysis engineer to purchasing department.
Introduce value engineering to new product development, and to process development.
Reduce labour costs: reducing frequency of performing the task.
    identifying the highly productive tasks.
    change equipment or personnel.
    eliminate idle time.
    eliminate overlapping work.
    eliminate duplicate work.
    eliminate overtime.
    establish standards of performance.
Use less space by condensing operations.
Apply method and work study to activities.
Cut plant and space costs.
Cut indirect salaries and wages; engineering, other services.
Replace fixed costs with flexible costs: use outside services instead of high cost internal services.
Apply job enrichment programme to work.
Apply productivity bargaining: incentive schemes.
    wage structure reform.

job evaluation.
fixed term contracts.
labour flexibility and mobility.
change working methods.

The product mix:

Cut high risk, high capital projects.
Narrow the range of products, improve the flexibility of sales/production.
Invest in appreciating assets.
Make use of short term and long term profit opportunities thrown up by inflation on: existing product range.
  future product range.
Develop radical new product ideas to launch when the market demand is turning up.
Measure impact of inflation on all aspects of product ranges: supplies, labour, distribution, customers, end users.
Develop low-cost, low-risk products.
Develop overseas markets.
Eliminate poor profit producers.
Profit strip weak products: cut packaging costs.
  cut sales costs.
  cut production labour.
  cut stockholding.
  cut servicing and spare parts.
  cut materials cost.
  widen quality control limits.
  raise the price.
  cut the discounts.
  cut promotion and advertising.
  degrade the quality.
Sell assets of discontinued lines: brand names.
  plant.
  product formulations.
  market data.
  patents.
Apply promotional resources behind high profit producers.
Apply promotional resources to products with high overhead productivity ratios, high net profits from limited fixed costs.
Reduce market segmentation.
Reduce marginal product innovations.
With price constrained product, drop it from range and produce one new one above the price and one new one below the price at lower quality.

Marketing operations:

Cut advertising costs, particularly advertising production.
Change advertising media mix.
Change advertising appeal.
Reduce sales promotion costs.
Change sales promotions to variable costs (offer incentives per case).
Provide greater flexibility to meet market changes.
Improve market information to identify changes in demand.
Carry out formal product tests.
Use inexpensive word-of-mouth promotion.
Increase product publicity levels.

Sales operation:

Adapt selling techniques for product shortages.
Improve sales productivity.
Reduce unwelcome customers.
Concentrate upon key accounts.
Develop new high volume accounts.
Improve customer development activity.
Reduce pre- and after-sales service levels.
Raise volume per order.
Raise order-to-call ratio.
Cut the total sales force size.
Change selling method to cheaper alternative.
Withdraw from uneconomic markets.
Expand into profitable new areas.
Increase products per order.
Reduce discounts per customer.
Provide customer incentives.
Change sales remuneration.
Improve sales training.
Introduce sales incentives.

Distribution and transport:

Reduce distribution points.
Use more central storage, fewer local depots.
Reduce delivery frequency.
Simplify total distribution system.
Reduce stockholding.
Speed stock flow.
Improve and standardise packaging.

Improve methods and procedures.
Speed up order processing.
Introduce technical improvements, automatic handling.
Change distribution channels.
Change distribution method for uneconomic areas.
Cut packaging costs.
Reduce storage space.
Cut labour costs.
Cut fixed costs.
Reduce indirect salaries and wages.
Use fewer vehicles, larger capacity.
Lengthen life of vehicles.
Reduce maintenance costs.
Use alternative transport methods: road (own vehicles)
    road (contract hire vehicles)
    rail
    sea
    air
Introduce collection by customers.

Appendix

Pricing Restrictions

In the present worldwide wave of inflation, governments have reacted, as they have in the past, by declaring inflation illegal. They have produced laws which, in varying degrees, forbid a rise in prices. The danger of this attitude is that price rises are only a symptom of a widespread disease. Governments usually hope that their policies will stave off inflation, maintain high employment and investment, and encourage economic initiative all at once. Price control has only marginally curbed inflation (particularly when, as now, much inflation is imported) and probably hinders the achievement of full employment, high investment and the beneficial use of economic initiative.

However, price controls are apparently the political policy to pursue during inflation and the voters would undoubtedly object to any government that failed to make a show of stopping price increases. Business has to live with government action and so this appendix describes some of the major features that are typical of price-control regimes and provides a brief survey of control action being taken around the world.

Typically, price controls are made increasingly severe as the rate of inflation increases. The initial legislation, usually exerted by governments when inflation runs at between 5—8 per cent, tends to be relatively mild, concentrating upon fiscal measures to regulate supply and demand. Interest rates go up, bank lending is cut short and so on. At rates between 8 and 10 per cent, governments tend to introduce price warning systems usually requiring the largest industrial companies to notify government departments of impending price increases and often to provide cost justifications.

The next stage in this escalation is for the government to 'permit' price increases before they are made. This happens when inflation is between 10 and 12 per cent. As a result companies within the same industry band together to present industry cases jointly to government departments. This action between competitive companies is only one step away from other agreements to share markets, to close off new competition, or to limit investment in new projects so as to secure profitability – all thoroughly unhealthy trends in a capitalist system.

Companies gradually seek ways around the restrictions imposed, which in turn must lead to more legislation which polices the companies more thoroughly. Some of the factors in this evasion and tightening-up game are:

1   Companies try to change the basis of their accounting procedures so that the pricing authorities cannot object to the case in any depth when presented with complicated and changing accounting bases.
2   Companies tend to yell before they are hurt, by putting in for price increases even though the new costs have not yet been incurred.
3   Some companies, restricted upon price, will then withdraw discounts and customer rebates.
4   Some companies reduce the amount of the product they will sell at a given price; or reduce the quality, making it inferior.
5   Some companies will drop one product and introduce a new one with a marginal difference in its features.
6   Some companies plead their case for price increases and government departments grant them, only to find the companies next declaring massive profits (possibly as a result of stock inflation). Politically, this is disastrous for governments so they then introduce legislation to control profits.

Rates of 12 per cent inflation and above begin to lead to social disorder and industrial aggravation as the population strives to maintain its standard of living against a discernible increase in living costs. What started out as imported inflation through higher-cost materials being brought into a country soon turns into a wage screw without end. Most advanced economies with a technological base find that a 20 per cent increase in labour costs will quickly push up prices by 10 per cent. But after a time lag, as the cost increases work their way through industry costs, the prices will be up by 14 per cent. Then there is the risk that this will drive up other costs, so that in the long run a 20 per cent increase in labour costs, by itself, can ultimately cause a 20 per cent increase in prices – the never-ending screw.

Standard provisions in most price codes

Most countries with inflation rates above 15 per cent have widespread price-control legislation, often with profit controls also. Some of the common features of such price codes are:

1   Companies are generally allowed to increase their prices by the amount of increase in certain allowable costs such as materials, components, supplies, fuel etc. A pay rise for staff, if it is in line with any wage-control legislation usually, can be partially reflected in price increases, on a sliding scale depending upon the potential for productivity increases.
2   Some prices are exempted from the restrictions including the first sale of imported goods, fresh foods, auction prices, taxi fares.
3   The largest companies must notify the authorities in advance of any price increase and in many countries they must present their trading and costing figures regularly for inspection.
4   Smaller companies are required to follow the provisions of the pricing legislation and their records may be inspected at any time.
5   Export prices are always excluded from the provisions and companies are urged to make as much profit and sell as much volume at as high a price as possible to overseas customers. This therefore reduces the capacity of the overseas country to deal with its own inflation. It, in turn, tries to export its inflation elsewhere — the never-ending international screw.

Some price controls around the world (Nov 1974)

Spain

The Council of Ministers must approve all price rises above 3 per cent for all industrial and consumer goods, while a Prices Board approves price increases up to 3 per cent. A full description of material, labour and overhead cost increases must be supplied. The price of new products and services introduced to the markets are to be compared with existing products and services before approval is granted. Productivity and profits records of each concern will be examined; margins must be 'justified'. Changes or falsifications in product quality, description, composition, or the stockpiling of materials or products may result in the establishment being closed. There are no controls over wage awards, and heavier taxes are being introduced into key sectors of industry.

Netherlands

Price increases are limited to the increases in costs since September 1973, with one-third of wage increases being allowed; service companies are limited by man-hours charged. Complete cost records for all products and services back to the base date of September 1973 must be maintained. Auctions and markets are generally excluded. One-month notification is required from all manufacturing firms whose turnover was above 1 million guilders in 1972.

Denmark

Cost increases in materials, goods, transport and service charges, public rates and duties, depreciation, authorized rent increases and wage increases may be reflected in price increases. The Monopolies Board may require an absolute ban on price increases at any time for a six-month period. Failure to comply results in fines or imprisonment or both. The Act does not apply to the Faroes or to Greenland who can fend for themselves as best they can, bearing in mind the rate of inflation in Iceland, their near neighbour, which is currently above 50 per cent a year.

Belgium

Three months' advance notification of price increases is required by the Ministry of Economic Affairs for all enterprises with a turnover above 5,000,000 francs. A wide range of goods have maximum prices established. Average margins within an industry are taken as guidelines. Penalties for infringement of the regulations may involve the closure of the enterprise. The first Belgian Price Commission was established as long ago as 1951.

Austria

Enterprises which do not pass savings of tax and duties in the form of lower prices may be summoned and their management imprisoned. Local authorities and the police enforce this section of the legislation.

Portugal

Maximum prices for certain goods are enforced; and others must be approved. Advance notification of justified price increases is required. Full and comprehensive price marking for goods is required.

United States

No price controls since 30 April, 1974.

Canada

No controls at present although discussion is proceeding and they may be enforced. The country is trying to contain inflation through an expansionist programme to increase the gross national product by 4 per cent a year.

France

There are several regulations covering price controls on specific products; the government is empowered to act in order to curb excessive profits. The government is encouraging saving through higher interest rates.

Australia

The Australian government at present has no power to control prices. However, the various states have offered the federal government this power in exchange for increases in state revenue paid to them. Higher taxes upon wage increases may be used to curb inflation which is forecast to go above 20 per cent in 1975.

Brazil

Through a system of indexing every aspect of private and public enterprise to a series of inflation 'norms', Brazil has managed to reduce her hyperinflation rate of up to 100 per cent down to 15 per cent. With the oil crisis inflation has crept back to 33 per cent. Every sector of the economy is controlled, however.

New Zealand

A compulsory savings scheme has been introduced to take some steam out of demand. Legislation on wage control is also planned for the future.

Index

Absenteeism and effect on increased
    output   87
Accounts' department, seven
    possibilities why it may be
    ineffective   68
    see also Financial accounting
Advertising:
    and marketing operations
    114–15
    do methods need changing?   13
Age and creativity   23
Agreements with outside companies,
    seven points to cover   54
Attribute listing, for profit
    improvement ideas   24–5

Bank, pay into, as soon as possible
    63
Brainstorming as a profit improvement
    idea   25–6
Budgeting to contain inflation
    48–51
Buyer:
    -awareness, creating   115
    behaviour model   80
    pricing strategy   127
    techniques:
        coercion   85
        inducement   85
        education   85–6
        persuasion   86

Capital bases, reduction of, to increase
    cash flow   65
Capital values and inflation   56
Cash discounts, taking advantage of
    63, 65
Cash flow:
    budget   63
    specimen table for forecasting
    64
Cash management, speeding the process
    of   63–4
    see also Financial accounting
Central costs, checking of   71–4
Checklist:
    for buying outside services   53–4
    for ideas to improve profits   25,
    149–55
Competition:
    meeting price-, 132–3
    and marketing costs   111
Computerised sales forecasting, a
    practical example of   46–7
Contracts, inflation escalation clauses
    in   131
Convergent thinking   23
Cost accounting process, unfreezing:
    check accounting department first:
        seven reasons for bad system
        there   68
    costing operations:
        materials   70
        labour   71

163

overheads and central costs
       71—4
    transfer pricing   74—5
    systematic approach   68—9
Cost-efficiency techniques   14—16
Cost-push   3
Cost-reduction and staff attitudes   17
Cost savings, do they increase costs
       elsewhere?   14
Cost value and increased output   89
Counter inflationary moves by
       improving product mix, *see*
       Product mix, improvement of,
       to counter inflation
Coverdale technique   21—2
Creativity defined   22—3, 24
Credit:
    negotiating   60—1, 63
    should it be made shorter?   13
    squeeze, effect of   3—4

Debtors, how to pursue for payment
       61—2
Decision-making unit for purchasing
       80—1
Demand pull   3, 5
Demarketing   8
Departmental costs, effects on, by
       changes in another's, *Table*   35
Depreciation and inflation   56
Direct costing and inflation   69
Director, duties of, classified by
       percentages, *Table*   47
Directors' responsibilities in
       organisational changes   45
Discounts:
    to meet price competition   132—3
    see also Cash discounts; Payment
       discounts
Distribution:
    checklist for improvement ideas
       and   154—5
    improving productivity in, *see* Sales,
       improving productivity in
Distribution costs, six opportunities
       to reduce   125

Distribution department, savings open
       to   34
Divergent thinking   23

Efficiency rather than growth?   88
Eliminating weak products   100—3,
       104—5
Esteem value and increased output
       89
Exchange value and increased output
       89—90

FIFO (first in, first out in warehousing)
       70
Financial accounting and cash
       management   55—65
    checklist for profit improvement
       ideas and   150—1
    inflation accounting   56—7
    how it works   57—9
    techniques with systematic
       approach:
       negotiating credit   60—1
       outstanding debts in sales
           61—3
       speeding up cash management
           63
       reducing capital base   65
Fixed cost and market down-turn
       when high   72

Growth or efficiency, which is
       better?   88

Historical costing and inflation   69
Holist and serialist approaches   26—7

Ideas for profit improvement:
    staff interrelation   19—21
    project methodology:
       thinking processes   22—4
       creative stimulus   24

attribute listing   24−5
forced relationships   25
morphological analysis   25
checklists   25, 149−55
brainstorming   25−6
synectics   26
determining profit through
    improved style   25−7
project team   21
Improved style, could it determine
    profit?   26−7
Industrial action, effect of, on
    increased output   87
Inflation:
    comparative rates of   3−4
    effects of, on companies when
        continuous   55
    escalation clauses in contracts
        131
    how it distorts business:
        general problem   3−9
        from shortages   7−9
        effects summarised   9
        when government interferes
            9−10
Inflation-accounting and how it works
    56−9
Inflation Spiral, Accounting for the
    (Platt)   57
Interactive effect   33−4, 36
Invoicing, speeding process of   63

Job enrichment and increased output
    93−4

Labour:
    costs of, checking   71
    efficiency, can it be improved?
        12
    increasing productivity of   91−4
        five areas where cuts can be made
            92
LIFO (Last in, first out in warehousing)
    70
Losses, example of how easily to make
    128

Management:
    audit   51−2
    check list for, and profit
        improvement ideas   149−50
    effectiveness, evaluation of   46−8
    objectives system (MBO)   50−1
    service costs, how to reduce
        52−3
    three factors required of   6−7
Managers, interrelation of, need for
    19
Marginal costing and inflation   69
Market:
    down turn of and high fixed costs
        72
    planning   116−18:
        four major weaknesses of   116
    research   112−14
Marketing operations:
    checklist for improvement ideas and
        154
    marketing costs and profit
        improvement   111−16
        market research   112−14
        advertising and promotion
            114−15
        market planning   116−18
        overhead costs of   117−18
Materials:
    costing, checking of   70
    shortage of, and inflation   7−9
    see also Shortages
MBO system   50−1
Morphological analysis as a profit
    improvement idea   25

New products, development of
    107−9

Objective setting, in market planning
    116
Oil crisis, effect of   7
Operating costs, checking of   69−70
Operations, adapting market, *see*
    Marketing operations

Organisational changes, four effects of
        19–20
Organisational structures, ten key
        questions on   44
Organisation: where weaknesses occur
        44–5
Output, increasing value of:
        improved human resources   93
        job enrichment   93–4
        labour productivity   91
        productivity bargaining   15, 94
        value analysis   88–91
                introduction of   90–1
                control of programme   91
Outside services, checklist for purchase
        of   53–4
Overheads costing, checking of
        71–4
        and market planning   116–18

Payment discounts, advantage to be
        taken of   63, 65
Press releases in advertising   115
Price:
        codes   158–9
        controls by governments   157,
        159
        ought it to be increased?   13
        reductions, seven rules for   135
        rises, nine rules governing   135
Pricing, checklist for profit
        improvement ideas on   150
Pricing plan, eleven chief factors in
        129
Pricing strategy and inflation:
        how to make losses with ease   128
        making price changes   133–5
        meeting price competition   132–3
        table of prices cut *vis-à-vis* increased
                production   134
Productivity:
        and cost reduction   14–15
        bargaining, effects of   15
        bargaining and increased output
                94–5

Product mix:
        checklist for production
                improvement ideas and
                153–4
        improvement of, to counter
                inflation   97–109:
                re-organisation and stock-market
                        investment   100–3
                profit stripping marginal profits
                        103–4
                product elimination   104–5
                new product development
                        107–9
Product publicity campaigns   115
Production, checklist for profit
        improvement ideas and   152–3
Products:
        development of new   107–9
        elimination of weak   100–3,
                104–5
        evaluating: fourteen points to
                consider   103
        planning of   98–109
        should new be developed or size
                reduced?   12
Profitability, five main areas for
        improvement in   44
Profit:
        before taxation, adjustment of, and
                inflation   58–9
        improvement:
                and marketing costs   111–16
                checklists for   149–55
                in general management   44–54
                        (organisation structures, 44–5;
                        management system and
                        routine, 45; evaluation,
                        46–8; tighter budgeting,
                        48–51; management audit,
                        51–2; reducing costs,
                        52–3)
                main steps to be taken
                        139–45
                outside purchase, checklist for
                        buying   53–4
                systematic approach to   11–17
                        (items to consider, 12–13;

standard cost-efficiency
techniques, 14—16;
productivity and cost
reduction, 14—15; value
analysis, 15; teams for,
15—16, 139—45;
employees' attitude, 17)
teams   15—16, 139—45
where to look for   29—40
    (three methods open, 29;
    cumulative improvements,
    effect of, 31—3; interactive
    savings, 33—6; re-
    organisation, departmental
    trade-offs, 37; marginal
    costs and opportunities,
    38—9; main profit making
    opportunities, 39—40)
Profit increase of 50%, table showing
    how achieved   30
Profit stripping   100—4
Project methodology, *see* Ideas for
    profit improvement
Project teams   21
Promotion and marketing operations
    114—15
Proportional demand basis in
    marketing   117
Purchasing, checklist for profit
    improvement ideas and   151—2
Purchasing department, savings open
    to   34
Purchasing operation, how to improve:
    buyer behaviour model   80
    decision making unit   80—1
    its effectiveness   79
    supplier evaluation   82—3
    supplier development   83—4
    strategies when supplies are short
        84—6; *see also* Buyer;
        Shortages
    task approach of   81—2

Queueing time, a source of waste
    46

Raw materials, could cheaper ones be
    found?   13
Recruitment, problems of, and
    increased output   87
Re-organisation as a way to improve
    profit   36—7
Retail Price Index, chart of changes in
    5
Rhodesia: example of changed market
    in, following UDI   11—14

Sales:
    distribution   123—5:
        seven aspects to study   124
        costs of   125
    effectiveness of, a practical example
        of how to study   123
    force, should it be reduced?   12
    fourteen points to study to improve
        121
    improving productivity in
        119—25:
        strategy during shortages
            119—21
        key customers   120
        long term planning   121
    long-term planning for   121
    operations, checklist for
        improvement ideas and
        154
Scanning and thinking   23—4
Seasonal demand and inflationary
    costs   113
Self-help schemes for customers when
    advertising   115
Serialist and holist approaches   26—7
Shortage of supply, buying strategies
    during   84—6
Shortages:
    announcing anticipated, as a sales
        technique   118
    impact on sales department of
        119—20
    in materials, effects of   9
Situation analysis in market planning
    116

Staff:
    problems of, when introducing a
        cost reduction programme
        17
    interrelation by   19—21
Standard costing, checking of   70
Statements, speeding the process for
        issuing   63
Stock-market investment   100—3
Strikes and effect on increased output
        87
Substitution of supplies   9
Supplier development   9
    when purchasing   83—4
Supplier evaluation in purchasing
        82—3
Synectics as a profit improvement idea
        26

Task approach to buying   81—2
Telephone, use of, as a sales weapon
        122

Trade-offs   37—8
Transfer pricing   74—5
Transport, checklist for improvement
        ideas and   154—5

Use value and increased output   89

Value analysis   15
    to increase output value   89—91
        the twelve questions to ask
        89—90
Variable discounts   132—3

Wages, demand for increased, and
        effects on output   87
Warehousing, can a better system be
        devised?   13
    see also Distribution